GHANA

in Pictures

VGS

Yvette La Pierre

Lerner Publications Company

Contents

INTRODUCTION ... 4

THE LAND ... 8
► Topography. Rivers and Lakes. Climate. Flora and Fauna. Natural Resources. Cities.

HISTORY AND GOVERNMENT ... 20
► Ancient Kingdoms. Early Migrants. Arrival of Europeans. The Slave Trade. Asante Kingdom. The End of Slavery and the Beginnings of British Control. British Crown Colony of the Gold Coast. Toward Independence. Nkrumah's Rule. Succession of Governments. Rawlings. President Kufuor. Government.

THE PEOPLE ... 36
► Ethnic Mixture. Health. HIV/AIDS. Education.

Website address: www.lernerbooks.com

Lerner Publications Company
A division of Lerner Publishing Group
241 First Avenue North
Minneapolis, MN 55401 U.S.A.

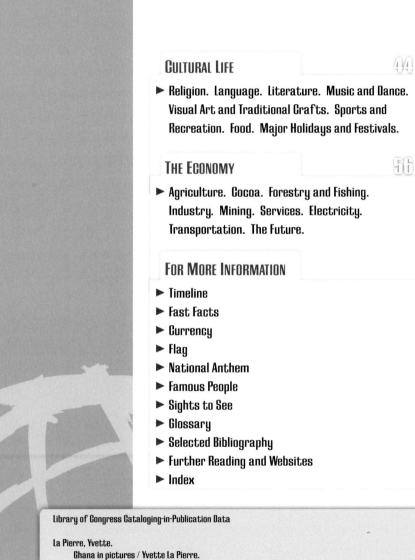

web enhanced @ www.vgsbooks.com

CULTURAL LIFE 44

► Religion. Language. Literature. Music and Dance. Visual Art and Traditional Crafts. Sports and Recreation. Food. Major Holidays and Festivals.

THE ECONOMY 56

► Agriculture. Cocoa. Forestry and Fishing. Industry. Mining. Services. Electricity. Transportation. The Future.

FOR MORE INFORMATION

► Timeline 66
► Fast Facts 68
► Currency 68
► Flag 69
► National Anthem 69
► Famous People 70
► Sights to See 72
► Glossary 73
► Selected Bibliography 74
► Further Reading and Websites 76
► Index 78

Library of Congress Cataloging-in-Publication Data

La Pierre, Yvette.
    Ghana in pictures / Yvette La Pierre.
        p.   cm. – (Visual geography series)
    Includes bibliographical references (p.) and index.
    Summary: Introduces through text and photographs the land, history, government, people, and economy of Ghana.
    ISBN: 0-8225-1997-6 (lib. bdg. : alk. paper)
    1. Ghana—Juvenile literature. 2. Ghana—Pictorial works—Juvenile literature. [1. Ghana.] I. Title.
II. Series: Visual geography series (Minneapolis, Minn.)
DT510.137 2004
966.7—dc22   2003022960

Manufactured in the United States of America
1 2 3 4 5 6 – BP – 09 08 07 06 05 04

INTRODUCTION

The West African nation of Ghana lies on the Gulf of Guinea between Ivory Coast and Togo. The people of Ghana named their country for the ancient Ghana Kingdom, which existed nearly five hundred years before the first Europeans reached the shoreline of present-day Ghana in 1471. When the Europeans arrived, they named the region "the Gold Coast."

As the name suggests, the Gold Coast had plentiful gold mines. One of Ghana's largest ethnic groups, the Asante, specialized in mining the precious metal. They were also famous for their skill at creating jewelry and decorative objects out of gold.

Many Europeans traveled to the Gold Coast to find the famous Asante gold, and later, they also came in search of slaves. Thousands of slaves were transported from the Gold Coast to Europe and America between the 1500s and the 1800s. Eventually, after great resistance from the Africans, the British gained control of the entire land. While the people of the Gold Coast were deeply influenced by the slave trade

and British rule, they also retained a strong sense of their own culture and had high hopes for independence.

In 1957 Ghana became the first country in colonial Africa to gain independence. It became an example for other colonies and seemed poised to become a leader among African nations. But independence was the start of serious economic decline and political instability. A long string of coups (sudden, often violent overthrows of a government) resulted in multiple dictators who provided weak leadership for the country. Yet despite economic and political difficulties, Ghana's people retained their strong spirit and hopes for a bright future, one that would match the glory of the kingdom of ancient Ghana.

Ghana is a land of great diversity. It is home to more than one hundred different ethnic groups. Its people have religious beliefs that include traditional religions, as well as Christianity and Islam. While Accra, Ghana's capital, contains high-rise buildings, Internet cafés, and a large soccer stadium, it also has large outdoor markets where

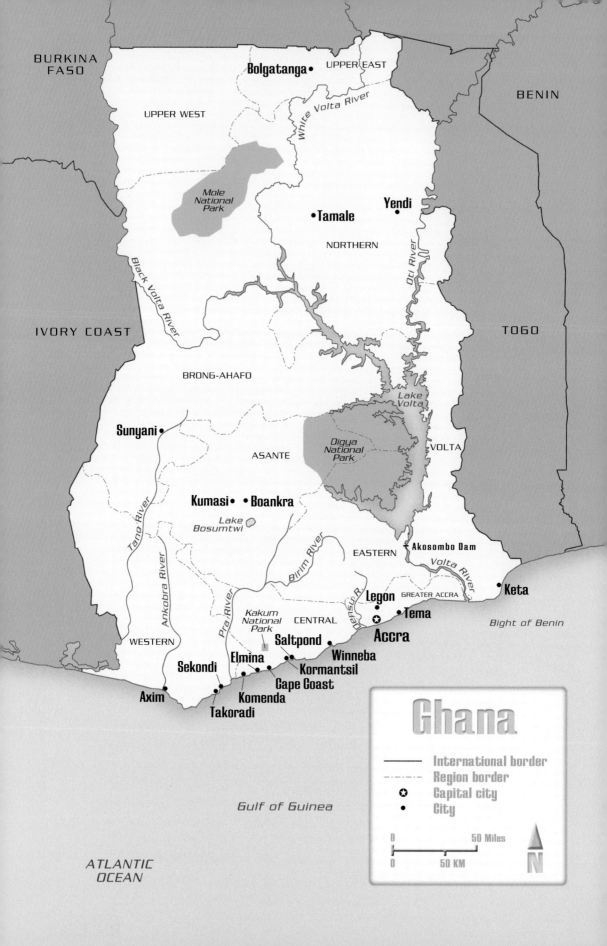

men and women sell traditional crafts, such as kente cloth. Many rural Ghanaians make their living by raising cacao trees, which provide beans for making chocolate. In addition, the land remains rich in gold, and gold and cocoa beans are two of the country's top exports.

Yet despite Ghana's rich natural resources, the country faces ongoing difficulties. In the early 1990s, the reign of dictators ended and the nation made a peaceful transition to democracy. The government and Ghanaian citizens faced economic problems including extreme debt, a high unemployment rate, and a low standard of living. Even so, the country has a per capita income two times higher than that of some of its neighbors. Ghana must continue to introduce political, social, and economic reforms to raise the standard of living for all of its people and live up to its potential as a leader among African nations.

Kente cloth received its name from the Asante term *kenten*, which means "basket," because of the cloth's resemblance to the woven design of a basket.

THE LAND

The small nation of Ghana lies in the center of the West African coast, about 400 miles (644 kilometers) north of the equator. On a map, the country is shaped like a tall, narrow rectangle and covers 92,100 square miles (238,537 square km), an area slightly smaller than the state of Oregon.

The Gulf of Guinea forms Ghana's southern border, and beyond the gulf is the Atlantic Ocean. Three French-speaking nations form its other three borders: Ivory Coast to the west, Togo to the east, and Burkina Faso to the north. Beyond Burkina Faso to the north and east are the vast, dry plains of the Sahel region and the Sahara Desert.

Topography

From the coast northward, Ghana can be divided into three distinct geographical regions: coastal plain, forests, and savanna. The country is bisected by a ridge of land called the Kwahu Plateau that runs diagonally from the southwest to the southeast.

The long, low coastal plain in southern Ghana has an average elevation of just 246 feet (75 meters) above sea level. The coast is pounded by heavy surf, and the water is dangerous. Despite its 335 miles (539 km) of coastline, Ghana has no natural harbors. The coastal soil is rich and the rain is plentiful, allowing farmers in southern Ghana to grow many crops, including bananas, sugar, corn, coffee, and cassava. Most of the country's population is concentrated in this fertile southern region.

North of the coast and to the southwest of the Kwahu Plateau lies the forest. The land rolls gently with small hills and broad, flat valleys. Mahogany, ebony, and other valuable trees grow in the forest, and farmers plant cacao here. In the extreme southwestern corner of the forested region, a tropical rain forest grows. It is characterized by heavy rainfall and broad-leaved evergreen trees that form a continuous canopy high above the forest floor.

The forest and the Kwahu Plateau are together sometimes called the Asante Uplands. To the north and east of these Uplands lies the

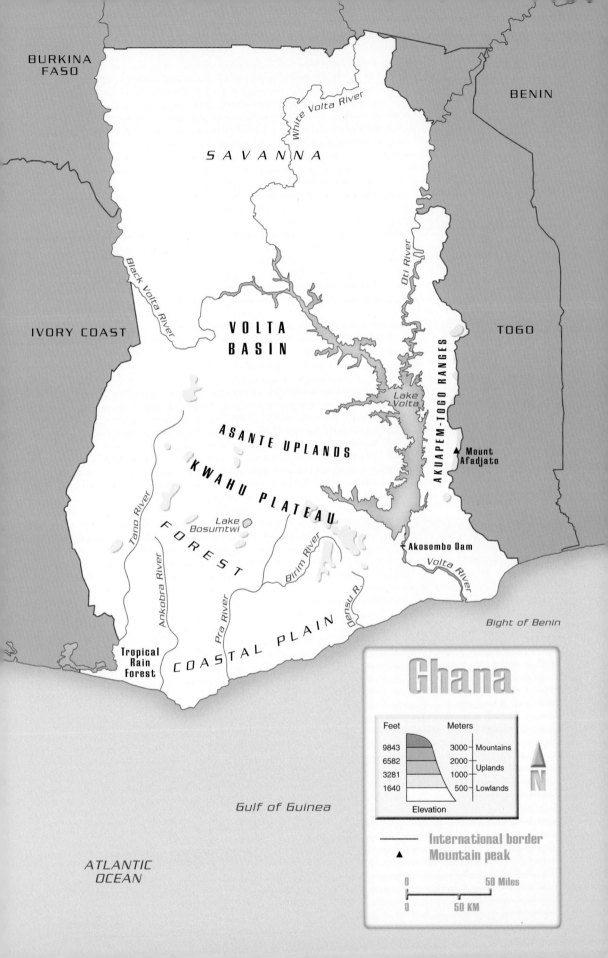

Volta river system—the Volta and its tributaries. All of the land drained by this river system is known as the Volta Basin. East of the Volta River, the land rises sharply to form the Akuapem-Togo ranges. Mount Afadjato, the highest point in Ghana at 2,905 feet (855 m), is in these ranges, which form the border with Togo.

Much of central and northern Ghana is savanna, dry grassy plains with a few bushes and widely spaced trees. This land is dry much of the year, though some parts are swampy in the rainy season. Northern Ghana is the least populated part of the country.

◐ Rivers and Lakes

Almost all the rivers and streams northeast of the Kwahu Plateau empty into the Volta River, which flows in a generally southward direction across Ghana and empties into the Gulf of Guinea between Tema and Keta. The Volta is Ghana's longest river, and its tributaries include the Black Volta, the White Volta, and the Oti. In the 1960s, a large dam was built on the Volta to generate electricity for the country. The Akosombo Dam backed up the Volta waters for 250 miles (402 km) to form Lake Volta, one of the world's largest artificially created

Fishers catch African pike and catfish on the upper **White Volta River,** a branch of Ghana's Volta River system.

Created by the Akosombo Dam, **Lake Volta** is one of Ghana's most important sources of freshwater.

lakes, with a surface area of 3,275 square miles (8,482 sq. km). About eighty thousand people had to be resettled from small communities along the river where their families had lived for generations.

In the north of Ghana, many rivers are seasonal. They may dry up completely during the dry season and flood during the rainy season. To the southwest of the Kwahu Plateau are several rivers that are independent of the Volta system. The most important of these are the Pra, Tano, Ankobra, Birim, and Densu rivers, which flow into the Gulf of Guinea.

Ghana has only one natural lake, Bosumtwi, near the city of Kumasi in south central Ghana. The lake is almost perfectly round and lies in a crater that may have been formed by volcanic activity. Along Ghana's coast are many marshes, mangrove swamps, inlets, and lagoons.

Climate

Ghana has a warm and humid climate typical of the tropics, a warm region near the equator. But climatic conditions change across the country and with the seasons. The country can be divided into two broad climatic zones: a hot and dry north and a generally hot and humid south. The southeastern coastal area is drier than the rest of the south.

Temperatures throughout the country are highest in the months of February and March, when they can reach above 100°F (38°C). Generally, the temperatures hover in the mid-80s (28° to 30°C). The country's average annual temperature is 79°F (26°C).

The area north of the Kwahu Plateau has two distinct seasons. From November to April is the harmattan season, when dusty winds from the Saharan region to the north bring hot, dry days and cooler nights. This is followed by the wet season, during which northern farmers plant and harvest their crops.

To the south and southwest of the plateau are four separate seasons. Heavy rains fall from about March to July. After a relatively short dry period in August, the rains start again, lasting from September to November. Then the harmattan season hits, lasting until February or March. Most of Ghana receives 40 to 60 inches (102 to 152 centimeters) of rain a year, though parts of the southwest receive more than 100 inches (254 cm).

Ghana's coastal cities often flood in June and July, at the peak of the rainy season. In 2001 flash floods in Accra displaced an estimated 100,000 people.

Flora and Fauna

Ghana's broad climatic zones support very different types of vegetation. Along the dry, narrow coastline to the east of the city of Takoradi, the vegetation is coastal savanna, a combination of tall grasses and low-growing trees and bushes. A few trees thrive in this region, including the ancient baobab tree. Anthills—some as tall as 10 feet (3 m)—are common, and plants form clumps around them.

Along the coast in the southwestern tip of the country, where there is more rain, tropical rain forests cover the land. Most of the trees are

Although much of Ghana is dry, **tropical rain forests like this one** thrive in the extreme southwest where rainfall is high.

evergreens. To the north and east of the tropical zone where rainfall is lower, the forest is filled with deciduous trees that lose their leaves in the dry season. Most of this area is secondary forest, or land that was logged and then grown over with new trees.

Hyena

In the northern savanna, long grass covers the ground, growing as high as 10 feet (3 m). Trees such as the baobab, acacia, and shea dot the landscape.

A rich array of wildlife lives in the varied environments of Ghana. The country has more than two hundred species of mammals, including elephants, leopards, monkeys, hyenas, and antelopes. Crocodiles and hippopotamuses are found in and around rivers. Brilliantly colored butterflies and more than three hundred bird species, including eagles, herons, and parrots, fill the skies. Ghana's many reptiles include two of the world's most dangerous snakes—the Egyptian cobra and the black mamba. Ghana's rivers, lakes, and coast support large numbers of fish, ranging from herring to flying fish to sharks.

In an effort to protect its forests and wildlife from logging and poaching (illegal hunting), Ghana has designated a system of parks, preserves, and sanctuaries where cutting down trees or hunting animals is regulated or prohibited. A highlight of the system is Kakum National Park, which boasts a skywalk—a long, narrow walkway strung high off the ground where visitors can get a bird's-eye view of the tropical rain forest

Kakum National Park's skywalk system allows visitors to walk more than 75 feet (23 m) above the ground in the tropical rain forest's upper levels.

canopy. The park's dense vegetation protects forest elephants, monkeys, yellow-backed duikers (small antelopes), and bongo antelopes. Digya National Park, one of Ghana's largest protected areas, is home to hippos, crocodiles, water buck, and manatees. Mole National Park is known for its lions, leopards, and many birds.

Natural Resources

Ghana is well endowed with natural resources. Valuable hardwood trees grow in the forests. The forested region also contains concentrations of minerals, including gold; diamonds; bauxite, the source of aluminum; and manganese, an ingredient for steel. The Ghanaian coast and interior waters offer rich fishing as well as a source of hydropower.

Cocoa, the raw ingredient of chocolate, is Ghana's leading export. It is not native to the area, however, and over the years much of Ghana's natural forests have been cut down to make room for cacao trees.

Ghana's forests are also under increasing pressure from the country's growing population and its needs for timber and farmland. Between 1981 and 1985, more than 54,000 acres (21,850 hectares) of forest were cut down each year. This deforestation (loss of forest) leads

The trees in this area near Kumasi were cut down to make room for a banana plantation. **Deforestation** destroys the habitat of Ghana's plant and animal species.

to erosion, as fertile topsoil that was once held in place by tree roots is washed away by rain or blown away by wind. The result is less fertile land, which leads to lower crop yields and increased poverty. The northern savanna is also subject to erosion from overgrazing by cattle, sheep, and other domestic animals.

Deforestation and habitat loss, as well as poaching, are also taking a toll on Ghana's wildlife. Large herds of elephants once roamed the land, but hunters killed many for their valuable ivory tusks. Lions and leopards have been mostly driven off by farmers. The Miss Waldron's red colobus monkey, which used to roam the woods of eastern Ivory Coast and western Ghana in noisy packs, appears to be extinct. If so, it would be the first loss of a primate in one hundred years.

Cities

Most major Ghanaian towns and cities developed from ancient trading centers, which were usually located at a crossroads or river crossing. Others grew around key mining sites or productive agricultural areas. The largest city is Accra, the capital. Important secondary cities include Kumasi, Tamale, Tema, Sekondi, and Takoradi.

Though Ghana is primarily an agricultural nation, 37 percent of its people live in urban areas. That's up from about 33 percent in 1990, which shows that an increasing number of Ghanaians are choosing to live in cities, rather than in rural areas. Jobs are scarce in rural Ghana, so many people come from the villages to find work in the cities.

ACCRA Approximately 1.9 million people live in the greater Accra area. As the capital, Accra is the political and administrative headquarters of the country. It was founded as a village of the Ga people, one of Ghana's ethnic groups, in the 1400s. Due to its coastal location, Accra grew into a prosperous trading center when Europeans began to arrive, eventually becoming the center of the African slave trade. In 1876 Accra became the administrative center for the British, who controlled much of the Gold Coast at that time. Christiansborg Castle, also known as Osu Castle, has served as government headquarters since then and is the official residence of the president of Ghana. In 1923 a new railroad linked Accra with the interior so that more goods could be transported to and from the city.

Twenty-first century Accra is a lively city where modern high-rises mix with small mud houses, and Ghanaians in business suits mingle with those in traditional clothes on the busy streets. Residents can shop in an open-air market, visit a cyber café, sit down at a "chop bar" (an inexpensive café) for delicious soups and stews, and spend leisure time at the soccer stadium and racecourse.

Independence Square, also known as Black Star Square, is the center of cultural activities. The Eternal Flame of African Liberation always burns there as a tribute to Ghana's freedom. Accra is home to the University of Ghana, the Accra Arts Council, several hospitals, a medical school, and an international airport. The main industries are tile and brick production and lumber and diamond processing.

Accra's Black Star Square includes the Freedom and Justice Arch *(background)*, the Eternal Flame of African Liberation *(center left)*, and the Tomb of the Unknown Soldier *(left)*. The square was built to commemorate Ghana's independence from colonial rule in 1957.

A bustling intersection in **downtown Kumasi**

KUMASI Lying in south-central Ghana, Kumasi the country's second-largest city, with close to 400,000 people. Considered the garden city of West Africa, it is a flower-filled city carved out of the jungle. Kumasi was founded in 1695 as the seat of the Asante Empire.

Kumasi remains a center of cultural life for the Asante people. The Asante king, the asantehene, lives there in the Manhyia Palace. During festivals, the palace is crowded with guests, and the streets are filled with people celebrating. The National Culture Centre includes a museum of Asante history with many items used by ancient Asante kings.

Kumasi is also the center of the gold-mining and the cacao-growing regions, which bring in most of the city's wealth. It boasts the largest open-air market in Ghana—and one of the largest in West Africa—where Ghanaians can shop for everything from fresh produce to auto parts. The city is also home to Kumasi University and other colleges and research institutions.

Vendors and customers haggle over prices at **Kumasi's open-air market.**

Situated on the Gulf of Guinea, **Tema** has become one of Ghana's most important ports. To learn more about Ghana's cities, climate, and population, go to vgsbooks.com.

SECONDARY CITIES Tema is located just east of Accra. It is Ghana's fourth-largest city and its second-largest port. Its population has grown from about 35,000 in the late 1950s to more than 110,000 since a new harbor was built there in 1960. Tema has a thriving fishing port, central market, and commercial area. Many cocoa warehouses and processing plants are located in Tema. Takoradi and Tema are the only Ghanaian cities on the Gulf of Guinea with deepwater ports to accommodate large oceangoing ships.

The twin cities of Sekondi and Takoradi lie just a few miles apart on the coast to the west of Accra. They are two separate cities, but because they are so close, they are often treated as one. Together they are the fifth-largest city in Ghana, with a population of about 103,000. Takoradi originated as a fishing village but has grown to become Ghana's largest port after an artificial harbor was built there in 1928. Sekondi has served as an important naval base since colonial times and is the administrative capital of its region.

Other towns along the coast include Saltpond (pop. 12,500), Elmina (pop. 27,000), and Cape Coast (pop. 78,700), all of which were first established by European colonists. Cape Coast has many schools, colleges, and a university.

Tamale is the major town and administrative center of the north. It has a population of about 151,000. Other large northern towns include Yendi (pop. 50,800) and Bolgatanga (pop. 88,200). Most of Ghana's major cities and towns, however, are in the south.

HISTORY AND GOVERNMENT

Archaeologists excavating areas around Tema have discovered new evidence of permanent settlers dating back as far as thirty-five thousand years ago. This evidence upsets long-held theories that Ghana was settled just a few thousand years ago.

Close to the Black Volta River, archaeologists have also uncovered evidence of a group of people who lived there between 1700 and 1500 B.C. These people were members of the Kintampo culture. Little is known about them, but archaeological evidence suggests that people of the Kintampo culture introduced herding and agriculture to the area.

◉ Ancient Kingdoms

The modern Republic of Ghana is named after the ancient kingdom of Ghana, founded by the Soninke people in the Western Sudan (a region of West Africa). Ancient Ghana flourished from the fourth to the eleventh century A.D. It occupied the area between the Senegal and Niger rivers about 500 miles (805 km) north of present-day Ghana.

Some historians have suggested that groups of people from the ancient kingdom of Ghana migrated southward to escape rebellion or unrest and settled in the region of present-day Ghana, joining hunting and gathering people who originally lived there.

The actual name of the ancient empire was Wagadugu, and its ruler was called the "Ghana." This highly advanced empire controlled the gold trade between the mining areas to the south and the Saharan trade routes to the north. Arab camel caravans brought copper, salt, and dried fruits from North Africa to Ghana's markets, where they traded for gold, ivory, and slaves from regions south of the ancient kingdom of Ghana. In addition to material goods, the caravans brought new ideas, knowledge, and religious beliefs from the north. At the height of its power in the tenth century, Ghana had an efficient government, a strong army, and centers of learning. The empire included followers of traditional religious beliefs as well as Muslims, followers of the Islamic religion to the north.

Despite its position of power and prosperity, the Ghana Empire began to weaken when a group of Muslim reformers—called the Almoravids—attacked, eventually capturing Ghana in 1076. Many of its people were killed or forced to convert to Islam, and trade was severely disrupted. The empire was completely destroyed by the thirteenth century.

Early Migrants

Oral tradition suggests that most present-day Ghanaians are descended from groups of people who began migrating into the area in the 1200s, making up the more than one hundred separate ethnic groups in Ghana. The first migrant groups probably came down the rivers of the Volta Basin.

The earliest known states in what became Ghana were the Dagomba and Mamprusi kingdoms in the north. They flourished beginning in the fifteenth century. About that time, groups of Akan speakers, including the Asante and the Fante, migrated from the northwest savanna and established a series of small states from the central forest lands south to the coast. Other groups migrated from Benin and southern Nigeria. Mande people, who were Muslim, came from present-day Mali to establish themselves in the northern half of Ghana.

These migrations were due, in part, to the rise and fall of the ancient empires in the Western Sudan. These migrants brought their highly organized systems of trade and government with them to their new home.

Arrival of Europeans

In the middle of the fifteenth century, the Portuguese, with the support of Prince Henry the Navigator, went looking for the source of gold that had reached Europe by way of trade caravans across the Sahara. In 1471 the Portuguese explorers landed on the southwestern coast of what became Ghana. They knew they had found what they'd come looking for when they saw the abundance of gold jewelry worn by the powerful Asante kings of the Akan people. The Portuguese found so much gold dust in the area that they named it El Mina de Ouro, or "the gold mine." The Portuguese also began trading with the local people for ivory and pepper. The land eventually became known as Costa D'Oro, or Gold Coast.

News of the area's wealth spread. In 1481 King John II of Portugal sent a

In late 1481 or early 1482, a ship sailing to Elmina Castle included a then-unknown sailor—Christopher Columbus. He was impressed by the riches of the area and learned much about Atlantic winds along the way. He used this knowledge on his more famous voyage in 1492.

Elmina Castle was the first in a system of forts erected along the coast of Ghana by Portuguese traders.

special mission to the Gold Coast to build the first permanent European trading post. São Jorge Castle, later known as Elmina Castle, was finished in 1482. The Portuguese later built more forts along the coast. The forts were designed to store the gold while trading ships were away at sea.

For a century, the Portuguese controlled the European trade along the Gold Coast with no competition. The mines along the coast provided tremendous amounts of gold each year for the king of Portugal.

The fortunes made by Portuguese traders on the west coast of Africa did not go unnoticed by other European nations. The first to challenge Portugal's trade monopoly were the Dutch. They arrived in the late 1500s and built forts on the coast at Komenda and Kormantsil (also known as Fort Amsterdam). The Dutch captured Elmina Castle from the Portuguese in 1637, as well as the fort at Axim in 1642.

Soon the English, Danes, and Swedes arrived, all hoping to establish trade in gold and slaves. The European nations fought with each other, building forts and capturing those of their rivals. At one time, seventy-six forts lined the coast, an average of one every 4 miles (6.4 km). As Europeans plundered West Africa for slaves and gold and fought one another for control, they drastically changed the lives of Africans living throughout the region.

◉ The Slave Trade

The practice of slavery and slave trading existed in Africa long before European contact. Northern groups conducted slave raids into West

Ghanaians who were captured for **the slave trade** were often forced to march for miles until they reached a major port or city.

Africa, and both men and women captured in local warfare became slaves. These slaves had specific rights, however, and many eventually became part of their masters' families.

Europeans, however, dramatically changed the scope and nature of slave trading. As Europeans established huge sugar, tobacco, and cotton plantations in North and South America, their demand for a cheap source of labor escalated. Soon the west coast of Africa became the principal source of slaves for the plantations of the Americas.

The Portuguese supplied Gold Coast tribes, including the Asante, with guns and gunpowder to encourage slave raids between tribes. The coastal tribes launched raiding parties into the interior of the country and brought back countless men, women, and children to the coastal forts to sell. Often they traded the slaves for more guns to become more powerful and take more slaves. The raiders took the healthiest and fittest people—the productive members of the village—leaving behind the very young, old, and weak to carry on.

The slaves were held in the prisonlike forts for a time. They were then loaded onto canoes with gold and other trade items to be transported to the ships that waited offshore, beyond the pounding surf. They were finally packed into the large vessels that would carry them across the Atlantic Ocean. The slaves were not treated well, and many died during capture or in the forts while awaiting shipment. Countless others died during the long ocean crossing to North and South America.

By the middle of the eighteenth century, slavery was the most important trade between Europeans and Africans. The slave traders did not keep exact records, but it is estimated that five thousand slaves were shipped from the Gold Coast every year, greatly disrupting local societies. Many African chiefs grew very rich by working with Europeans or by demanding bribes when trade routes crossed their territory. Others saw how destructive the trade in human beings was and tried to stop it.

Asante Kingdom

During the time of European influence and slave trading on the coast, the Asante Kingdom came to power in the interior of the country. The Asante Kingdom was the most powerful and influential of the Gold Coast's early kingdoms. In the late 1600s, an Akan chief named Osei Tutu united five smaller states and became the first asantehene of the Asante Kingdom. He built the Asante capital at Kumasi and established a golden stool as a symbol of his power. According to legend, the stool had floated down from the sky and it contained the soul of the Asante nation. Osei Tutu believed that if the Golden Stool were ever captured, the Asante Kingdom would lose their power.

Osei Tutu built a powerful army and began expanding his empire by conquering surrounding states. By the mid-1700s, most groups of Ghana's interior formed part of the Asante Kingdom. The last holdout was the Fante Empire of the coastal area, which controlled direct trade with the Europeans. Osei Tutu did not succeed in defeating the Fante, but after several bad kings, Asantehene Osei Bonsu and his armies defeated them in 1807. At its height in the early 1800s, the Asante Kingdom controlled an area similar in size to modern Ghana.

The End of Slavery and the Beginnings of British Control

In 1807 Britain's Parliament forbade British participation in the slave trade within the British Empire. Other nations, however, wanted to continue the lucrative trade and continued to sneak past the British warships posted along the African coast to turn back slave ships. Many African chiefs also objected to the abolishment of the slave trade, which had made them rich.

At the same time, the British, who hoped to colonize the Gold Coast, felt threatened by the growing power of the Asante Kingdom, with its well-organized government and powerful army. The Asante began to invade the coastal

THE GOLDEN STOOL

When the British learned that the Golden Stool held the strength of the Asante Kingdom, they demanded it be brought to them. The Asante fooled them with a fake gold-colored stool, which is on exhibit at the National Culture Centre in Kumasi. The Golden Stool is still a symbol of the king's power, and it is kept in the Manhyia Palace in Kumasi. The stool is so sacred that not even the king is allowed to sit on it, and it never touches the ground.

area, attacking the Fante and other ethnic groups in the region, as well as European forts. The Asante's goal was to gain access to the trading post at Elmina and take control of the trade between the interior and the coast. In an attempt to make peace with the Asante, the African Company of Merchants, which consisted of local British, Dutch, and Danish authorities, signed a treaty of friendship with the Asante in 1817. The treaty recognized Asante claims to sovereignty (control) over large areas of the coast and its people.

By the mid-1800s, many Christian missionaries were established in the Gold Coast, where they founded churches, schools, and hospitals.

In the 1850s, the Danes left the Gold Coast, leaving only the Dutch and British. In the 1860s, the slave trade finally ended. By 1872 the Dutch had also pulled out, leaving Britain the sole European power on the Gold Coast. Britain's only remaining challengers to control of the land were the Asante.

The British attacked Kumasi, the center of the Asante Kingdom in 1874, burning and looting the city. The British declared the lands from the coast to the Asante Kingdom a British Crown Colony of the Gold Coast. However, the Asante continued to resist British control, even as Britain explored and extended its power to territories to the north of the Asante lands. In 1877, as part of their increased involvement in the country, the British moved the seat of colonial administration from Cape Coast to Accra. The British finally defeated the Asante in 1901. The Asante Kingdom officially became part of the British protectorate (lands ruled by Britain) in 1902. At that time, the British controlled all three territories of the Gold Coast: the coast, the Asante lands, and the Northern Territories (a broad region north of the Asante lands).

British Crown Colony of the Gold Coast

The Asante and Fante had strong traditions of government and education that helped make the Gold Coast the showpiece of Britain's colonies. The British relied on tribal chiefs and their well-organized societies to explain and carry out the rules of the colonial government. Christian missionaries had established the first schools in the Gold Coast in the mid-1800s, and the British took control of many of these schools during the colonial period. The British made education more widely available, establishing secondary schools across the country. The colony was also rich in natural resources. As a result, the Gold Coast was the richest and best educated of Britain's African colonies.

Britain was most interested in profiting from these natural resources. The British built gold, manganese, bauxite, and diamond

An African in a European-style suit walks down Kumasi's main street in 1900. At that time, Kumasi had 3,000 inhabitants.

mines. They also introduced new crops to farmers, most notably the cacao tree.

Using local labor, the British built railways and roads to carry goods from the productive agricultural areas and mines to the coast. They dug harbors to collect the products for export to Britain. Towns grew around the transport hubs, and the British government built hospitals and more schools. Africans had improved access to education, clean water, sanitation, and energy sources. By World War I (1914–1919), the Gold Coast had the best schools, civil service, and legal system of the African colonies. A teacher's training college, Achimota College, was founded in Accra, though university education was not available in the country. Africans from the Gold Coast had to travel to Europe or America for higher education.

In return for all the development and increased infrastructure, British companies made huge profits from the labor and resources of the Gold Coast. The British gained more land in 1918, after World War I, when Germany lost one-third of the neighboring colony of Togoland to Britain. The area was renamed British Togoland, and it eventually became part of the Gold Coast colony.

Toward Independence

As Gold Coast Africans became more economically stable and better educated, they could see the inequity of the colonial system, which allowed the British government to exploit the people and resources of the Gold Coast to improve the lives of people in Britain. Africans could not choose their country's leader or take on positions of power in the government. Political parties dedicated to putting more control of the country in the hands of Africans began to emerge in the 1920s. Then, during World War II (1939–1945), Britain asked the people of the Gold Coast to join forces with them. The Africans fought bravely alongside British soldiers in several regions, including Ethiopia and Burma. But when the African veterans returned home, they were once again second-class citizens in their own country. After serving side by side with British soldiers, these Africans found it difficult to return to a society in which they did not have the same rights as the British.

In response to their demands for increased rights, the British began to grant Africans a little more power. In 1946 a new Gold Coast constitution was drafted, which resulted in Africans being elected to a majority in the Legislative Council for the first time. Despite this dramatic change, the British governor of the Gold Coast and his cabinet kept most of the power.

In 1947 the United Gold Coast Convention (UGCC) asked Kwame Nkrumah to be its general secretary. The UGCC was founded by lawyers and a wealthy businessman with the goal of African self-government for the Gold Coast. Nkrumah had trained as a teacher at Achimota College and had then left Ghana to study in the United States and Britain. In 1949, after serving as general secretary of the UGCC for two years, Nkrumah broke away from the UGCC to form his own party, the Convention People's Party (CPP). Its slogan was "Self-Government Now," and the party was aimed at ordinary

Kwame Nkrumah formed the Convention People's Party (CPP) in 1949. Find out more about Nkrumah, Ghana's first elected president, at vgsbooks.com.

working people, rather than the country's intellectual elite, the UGCC's focus. Nkrumah and his supporters led a national strike, nearly bringing the country to a halt. The British imprisoned Nkrumah in 1950 but released him the following year after his party won general elections by a landslide. The British governor of the Gold Coast, Sir Charles Arden-Clarke, appointed Nkrumah "leader of government business" (similar to prime minister). In 1952 Nkrumah was officially appointed prime minister and granted even greater responsibility for the country's future. Two years later, a constitution was formally adopted, and Gold Coast Africans ran their own government, except in the areas of external affairs, defense, and police.

At midnight on March 6, 1957, in the presence of Britain's Duchess of Kent, U.S. vice president Richard Nixon, U.S. civil rights leader Martin Luther King Jr., and other leaders, Britain's flag was lowered, and the red, green, gold, and black flag of Ghana was raised. Ghana, as it was renamed, became the first African country south of the Sahara to gain independence, with Nkrumah as its first prime minister. In July 1960, Ghanaians voted to enact a new constitution making Ghana a republic and elected Nkrumah to be their president.

Kwame Nkrumah *(center)* is **sworn in as the first president** of an independent Ghana in 1960.

PAN-AFRICANISM

Kwame Nkrumah believed Africans should ignore the country borders drawn by Europeans during the colonial period in Africa, which arbitrarily split ethnic groups among countries. The Pan-African movement maintained that Africa would be stronger if all Africans worked together. The movement continued long after Nkrumah's death. In July 2002, fifty-three African nations, including Ghana, launched the African Union. The main objective of this pan-African entity is to achieve greater unity among nations to improve the lives of all Africans.

◎ Nkrumah's Rule

Upon independence, Ghana had the benefit of a long history and a rich mix of cultures. It also had half a billion U.S. dollars in reserves and a strong economy based on its exports of gold and cocoa.

Nkrumah had fought long and hard to bring independence to Ghana, and he wanted to improve the living conditions of Ghanaians. To do so, Nkrumah declared himself president for life, banned all political parties except his own, and imprisoned his opponents. He thought these measures would allow him to more easily bring about changes he felt were necessary. Unfortunately, as Nkrumah's personal power grew, so did government corruption.

Nkrumah began to spend extravagantly—and then borrow from other countries—to finance his health, welfare, and education programs and large industrial projects such as the Akosombo Dam. Many of his projects did improve living conditions for some Ghanaians, but then the economy began to falter. Government debt and bad policies, along with falling world cocoa prices, crippled the economy. By 1966 Ghana was one billion dollars in debt, and corruption was widespread.

On February 24, 1966, while Nkrumah was on an official visit to China, Ghanaian army leaders seized power and arrested Nkrumah's supporters. The first republic and parliament were dissolved. The National Liberation Council (NLC), headed by Lieutenant General Joseph Ankrah, was formed to govern the country. Nkrumah did not return and, instead, took refuge in the West African country of Guinea, where he remained in exile until his death.

◎ Succession of Governments

Beginning in 1966, Ghana went through a succession of seven governments. Most of these governments were military, which meant that Ghanaians couldn't elect their own leaders.

In April 1969, Ankrah was replaced with Lieutenant General Akwasi Afrifa. Later that year, Ghana adopted a new constitution and held its first multiparty election since independence. Civilian rule returned with Kofi Busia of the Progress Party as prime minister and Edward Addo as president.

Military rule returned in January 1972, when Colonel Ignatius Acheampong took over as head of state. He was forced to resign in a coup led by another military leader, General Frederick Akuffo, in 1978. Akuffo said that he would hand over power to a popularly elected government on July 1, 1979. But before he could, the country was shaken by yet another coup in June, this one led by a group of young military officers. The Armed Forces Revolutionary Council (AFRC) was set up under the leadership of Flight Lieutenant Jerry Rawlings.

Rawlings

Rawlings vowed to uproot corruption in government and had Afrifa, Acheampong, and Akuffo executed for that offense. In July 1979, Rawlings allowed the previously scheduled elections to go on as planned. Ghanaians elected Hilla Limann as president, and Ghana returned to civilian rule in September of that year.

When corruption continued and economic conditions worsened under Limann, Rawlings staged another coup on December 31, 1981. This time he stayed in power. He dissolved the constitution and set up the Provisional National Defense Council (PNDC) with himself as its chairman and the effective ruler of Ghana.

Political revolutionary **Jerry Rawlings** *(center)* addresses a crowd in Accra shortly after the 1981 coup.

Rawlings imposed tight controls on government spending to help control inflation and attract financial aid from the United States and Europe, including support from the International Bank for Reconstruction and Development (World Bank). His government devalued Ghana's currency throughout the 1980s in order to stimulate exports. (Reducing the exchange value of Ghana's money made Ghanaian goods cheaper on the world market.) Though some Ghanaians benefited from these changes, many did not. In the 1980s, many Ghanaians lost their jobs. In addition, drought led to crop-damaging brush fires and food shortages. Many Ghanaians left home to work in Nigeria, but in 1983 the Nigerian government sent more than one million Ghanaians back home. As a result, food, water, and job shortages worsened. It was a time of curfews, government control of the press, and closed borders. The Rawlings-led government suppressed many coups during that decade.

Despite these problems, Ghana's economy gradually improved, in part because of a plan with the International Monetary Fund (IMF) and a move toward democratic reform. Throughout this era, the charismatic Rawlings was popular with many in Ghana.

In 1990 the National Commission for Democracy (NCD) organized forums throughout Ghana in which all Ghanaians could discuss what form of government they wanted for their country. The NCD found that the people wanted a multiparty system of government.

As a result, in 1992 a fourth constitution was passed, providing for a president elected by the people. Rawlings, running as a civilian, rather than as a member of the military, won the presidency in multiparty elections in November.

After ruling Ghana for more than ten years as the nation's self-proclaimed head of state, **Rawlings** was officially elected president in 1992.

In January 1993, Rawlings became the first president of the Fourth Republic of Ghana, and his party, the National Democratic Congress (NDC), won a vast majority of seats in Parliament. Rawlings was reelected in 1996 but, under Ghanaian law, was not allowed to seek a third term in 2000.

President Kufuor

On December 7, 2000, several candidates vied for the presidency. They included Vice President John Mills, chosen by Rawlings to succeed him, and John Kufuor of the opposition New Patriotic Party (NPP). When no candidate won the required 50 percent of the vote, another election was held between the top vote winners, Kufuor and Mills. Five minor candidates supported Kufuor, who won a landslide victory over the NDC in the second round. The NPP ended the NDC's control of the legislature, taking ninety-nine out of Parliament's two hundred seats, while the NDC won ninety-two seats.

Kufuor was sworn in as president on January 9, 2001. He pledged to work during his term to create the wealth needed for a healthy Ghana.

KOFI ANNAN

In 1997 a Ghanaian named Kofi Annan *(above)* was elected to the position of secretary-general of the United Nations. He became the first secretary-general from Africa south of the Sahara. In 2001 he and the United Nations were awarded the Nobel Peace Prize for their work combatting AIDS and international terrorism.

Visit vgsbooks.com, where you'll find links to biographies of Ghanaian leaders, historical facts, and government information.

John Kufuor flashes a victory sign at the crowd shortly after being sworn in as president of Ghana in 2001.

After fourteen years of civil war in nearby Liberia, Ghana helped forge a fragile cease-fire between the Liberian government and two rebel groups to move that country toward democratic elections. The cease-fire was signed in Accra in June 2003, and Ghana continued to host peace talks between the groups throughout the summer.

The road to democracy in Ghana has been bumpy. Since independence, however, Ghana has made great strides in improving the quality of life for its people and continues to institute more political, social, and economic reforms. In the early 2000s, Ghana has a relatively stable economy and government.

Government

The Constitution of the Fourth Republic of Ghana, was approved by a national vote on April 28, 1992. The constitution calls for a multiparty political system and divides power among a president, parliament, cabinet, council of state, and an independent judiciary.

The people elect the president to a four-year term and presidential tenure is limited to two terms. The president serves as head of state and commander in chief of the armed forces. The president appoints a cabinet to help carry out the functions of the government. A parliament, whose two hundred members are elected by the people to four-year terms, makes the country's laws.

Ghana is divided into ten regions with democratically elected local governments. Regions are divided into districts. Each district has its own district assembly.

The judicial system is based on common law (legal codes introduced by the British), traditional law, and the 1992 constitution. The judicial system consists of a supreme court (the highest court), court of appeal, and high court of justice. Under these are district, traditional, and local courts that apply laws at the local level.

In addition, all across Ghana local chiefs apply tribal laws and make decisions affecting the people in their care. Chiefs have the power to enact local laws as long as they do not contradict state and federal laws. These traditional government systems of tribal and village chiefs have survived through British rule and the succession of governments in Ghana.

Ghana's defense system consists of an army, navy, air force, police force, and civil defense (trained civilians who will help in emergency situations). The army is Ghana's largest and best-equipped defense system. During early independence, all military equipment and training came from Britain. After 1960 Ghana diversified its military relations to include China, the Soviet Union, East Germany, and Libya. In the 1990s, Ghana renewed military ties with Britain and forged new ones with the United States and other European countries. Ghana has also provided military units for United Nations (UN) peacekeeping operations.

THE PEOPLE

An estimated 19.9 million people live in Ghana, giving the country an overall population density of 216 people per square mile (83 people per sq. km). Seventy percent of the population lives in the southern half of the country. The most populous regions of the nation are the coastal area, the Asante region, and the two principal cities, Accra and Kumasi.

Ghana's population is growing at a rate of 2.3 percent per year. Like most developing countries, Ghana has a young population. Children 15 and younger make up 43 percent of the population, while only 3 percent are 65 years or older. The high percentage of young Ghanaians is expected to continue in the future as Ghanaian women each have an average of four children.

In spite of the considerable increase in urbanization in the 1980s and 1990s, Ghana remains largely rural. Close to 63 percent of Ghanaians live in rural areas in small villages. The typical one-room village home is made with mud or concrete walls and a tin roof. In rural areas, families are made up of grandparents, parents, children, aunts, uncles, and

cousins who live in a compound and share space for cooking and eating. The village may also contain the village well, a church or mosque (Muslim place of worship), an elementary school, a clinic, a market-place, and other public buildings. Beyond the village are the fields.

Most rural Ghanaians are farmers. Men raise crops, such as cacao, on small farms, and women raise food such as vegetables on small plots to feed their families. Most Ghanaian women work with men on the farm or on their own as traders as well as raising the family and tending the home. Children are expected to help out on the farm, and girls also help with housework and cooking. Many rural families don't have running water at home, so children spend a lot of time gathering water.

More and more Ghanaians are moving to cities to take advantage of government, manufacturing, and commercial jobs. Urban centers, such as Accra and Kumasi, have a wide range of living conditions. Prosperous Ghanaians live in large new homes with electricity, good sanitation, and plenty of electrical appliances such as televisions and

In a village near Kumasi, **three generations of this family live together** under the same roof. Extended families often share the same home.

refrigerators. Many middle-class city dwellers live in modest homes with a small yard or courtyard where they can keep a few chickens or perhaps a pig. Still others live in slums or shantytowns where there is no electricity, piped water, or sanitation system. Open sewers flow past the rickety buildings.

Ethnic Mixture

More than 99 percent of Ghana's people are sub-Saharan Africans (people native to Africa whose ancestors lived south of the Sahara Desert) belonging to approximately one hundred different ethnic groups. These groups include the Akan, Dagomba, Ewe, Guan, Ga-Adangbe, Wala, Builsa, and Dagaaba. These are further subdivided into numerous cultural and linguistic groups and subgroups. Less than 1 percent of Ghanaians are of European and Asian descent. Refugees from Liberia, Sierra Leone, and Togo also reside in Ghana.

THE AKAN PEOPLE are a large ethnic group, divided into subgroups who all speak dialects of the Twi language. The subgroups include the Asante (also spelled Ashanti), Fante (also spelled Fanti), Akuapem, Bono, and Nzema. Within the Akan, the most numerous peoples are the coastal Fante and the Asante of central Ghana. The Akan group accounts for nearly half of Ghana's total population.

Akan people excel in metalworking due to their long history in the gold trade. The original Akan territory contained one of the richest gold-fields in Africa. Africans from the north and Europeans came to Akan territory to trade for gold. Akan leaders grew rich and powerful on the trade and founded the Asante Kingdom. As the Asante Kingdom grew, it threatened the European gold- and slave-trading forts along the coast.

Asante woman

The Asante are the largest subgroup in Ghana and continue to be powerful in the 2000s. They are also one of the few matrilineal societies in Africa, which means that families trace their descent through the mother and her ancestors. Once known for the golden splendor of their rulers, modern Asante are most famous for their craft work, particularly carved stools and brightly colored kente cloth. Most make their living as farmers, and many raise cacao.

OTHER GROUPS The Ewe live in the Volta region in southeastern Ghana and make up about 13 percent of the population. They are farmers, fishermen, and blacksmiths.

The Accra plains are inhabited by the Ga-Adangbe, who make up 8 percent of the population and include the Ga, the Krobos, and the

Some **members of the Ewe group** practice voodoo, a religion that involves using music to communicate with ancestors. Here, worshipers hold a celebration in their village square.

Adas. Traditionally, the Ga were farmers, but modern Ga also fish and trade. In a Ga family, the traditional breadwinner is the woman.

The northern regions comprise many tribal groupings, including the Dagarti, the Sisala, the Mamprusi, the Konkomba, and the Frafra. Most northern Ghanaians, however, belong to the Mole-Dagbane group, which makes up about 16 percent of Ghana's total population. The Mole-Dagbane live in walled villages and work as farmers, growing sorghum, yam, millet, corn, and groundnuts (peanuts). They also raise cattle.

Health

The most common infectious diseases in Ghana include malaria, measles, onchocerciasis (river blindness), meningitis, schistosomiasis, tuberculosis, and typhoid. The government and healthcare workers have put a great deal of effort into combating these and other diseases.

An important objective of Kufuor's government is to ensure access to basic healthcare for all Ghanaians and to improve and enlarge the district hospital network. All regional and most district capitals have hospitals and clinics. Some villages and towns also have health centers. Ghana has major hospitals in Accra and Kumasi. In addition, a number of religious and private organizations operate hospitals and clinics throughout Ghana.

Ghana, however, does suffer from a shortage of hospital beds and doctors. The government is considering a package of incentives for doctors to improve their standard of living in hopes that they will stay in Ghana rather than choosing to work abroad. A free national health service is also being considered in Ghana. Healthcare is free for pregnant and nursing women, the elderly, psychiatric patients, patients with snake and dog bites, healthcare workers, tuberculosis patients, and children five and younger.

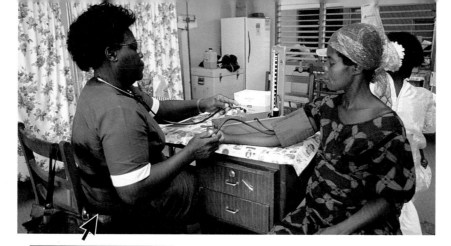

In **a health clinic near Accra,** a pregnant woman receives prenatal care.

Water management is another important aspect of Ghana's health-care. Many poor people in Ghana—in both rural areas and cities—do not have access to safe drinking water. Unsafe water can lead to the spread of diseases such as cholera, hepatitis A, and guinea worm. In addition, some parts of Ghana experience long periods of either torrential rain with flooding or severe drought, which can lead to disease and malnutrition.

Nonetheless, comparing health statistics from the 1960s and 1970s and the early 2000s indicates that Ghana made significant improvements

A child pours water into her family's cooking pot. Many Ghanaians do not have running water, and they must carry water from pumps and wells to their homes.

in heath care at the end of the twentieth century. The infant mortality rate—the number of babies who die within their first year—is 56 deaths per 1,000 live births, compared to 120 in 1965. Life expectancy at birth is about 57 years, up from a 1970 average of 44 years. Reasons for the improvements in infant mortality and life expectancy include an increase in government spending on healthcare, construction of more health centers in rural areas, widespread immunization programs against childhood diseases, and improved training for village health workers and traditional midwives (birth attendants).

HIV/AIDS

The human immunodeficiency virus/ acquired immunodeficiency syndrome epidemic is a serious problem in Ghana. The disease takes its heaviest toll in outlying rural communities and among people fifteen to forty-five years old, who are the economically productive sector of the nation.

More than 3.6 percent of the entire adult population is infected with HIV, the virus that causes AIDS. In 1999 about 340,000 Ghanaians were infected with HIV, 14,000 of whom were children. Since the epidemic began in the early 1980s, an estimated 33,000 Ghanaians have died from AIDS.

To control the continued spread of HIV, the government is working to promote the use of safe-sex behaviors, treat and control other sexually transmitted diseases, maintain a safe blood supply, and ensure safe use of hypodermic needles. The government is also striving to treat the problems of those already infected with the virus.

Education

Ghana has a good reputation for its well-developed education system. It has an overall adult literacy rate of 70.3 percent. In comparison, Ghana's neighbor, Burkina Faso, has a literacy rate of 19 percent, and Kenya in East Africa has the highest literacy rate on the continent at 78 percent.

Though a small number of children begin school at age three or four in preprimary or nursery schools, most Ghanaians begin school at five or six. Primary and secondary education is free between the ages of six and fourteen and is mandatory, though Ghana does not have teachers and facilities available to accommodate all students. Parents must pay for books, supplies, and required school uniforms. Because of these school fees, poor families cannot always afford to send their children to school. Ghanaian schoolchildren learn to read and write in English, the country's official language.

Students must pass a nationwide competitive exam organized by the West African Examination Council to enter secondary school, where they study math, English, science, social studies, and technical and vocational subjects for three years. After this level, students may choose to enter a technical or vocational institute or take a second exam to enter a three-year senior secondary school program. Students who complete this level may take another exam to go to a university. Higher education in Ghana is provided by the University of Ghana in Legon, Kwame Nkrumah University of Science and Technology in Kumasi, the University of Cape Coast, the University for Development Studies in Tamale, and the University College of Education in Winneba.

At the time of independence in 1957, Ghana had only a handful of secondary and primary schools and one university. By the early twenty-first century, Ghana had more than 13,000 primary schools, 6,400 junior secondary schools, 500 senior secondary schools, 20 teacher training colleges, 60 technical institutions, and 5 universities. From 1992 to 2002, Ghana spent between 28 and 40 percent of its annual budget on education.

Despite this, a significant number of those who are three years old or older have never been to school. In remote villages, the nearest school may be too far away, or children, especially girls, may be kept at home to help with chores.

Some **rural schools** do not have formal classrooms. Classes are often held outside.

CULTURAL LIFE

Modern Ghana is a rich mix of many distinct cultures and centuries of tradition. Ghanaians draw on the traditions of their ancestors for their art, music, and literature, for their festivals and ceremonies, and for their everyday lives.

◉ Religion

Ghanaians practice many religions, but the three main religions are animism, Islam, and Christianity. Mosques and churches of most major Christian denominations can be found in every region of Ghana. Ghana is a secular state, which means that the government does not officially support any particular religion.

In general, more people in the south are Christian, and more northern Ghanaians are Muslim. People throughout Ghana follow animist beliefs, and some Ghanaians practice a combination of Christianity or Islam and animism. In general, Ghanaians are respectful of the different religious beliefs of their neighbors and even their own family members.

ANIMISM About 40 percent of Ghana's population practice indigenous (local) religions. These religions are called animism. Though each ethnic group has its own set of beliefs, they all share common elements. Animists believe in a Supreme God who communicates with human beings through a host of lesser gods. People don't worship this Supreme Being directly because the being is thought to be too remote from daily life. The lesser gods are a part of the natural world, so all things—animals, plants, rocks, and trees—are respected and might be called upon for help through the intervention of a priest. Many village celebrations take place in honor of one or more deities (gods).

Animists also have great respect for their ancestors, who they believe watch over them and connect them to the spiritual world. People often build shrines to their ancestors. Family members give thanks to their deceased ancestors when something good happens, such as the birth of a baby, a new job, or a good harvest.

ISLAM Arab traders brought Islam to Ghana sometime around the fifteenth century. Islam was founded in seventh-century Arabia by the prophet Muhammad, and its followers are called Muslims. Muslims believe that Allah (God) sent many prophets (teachers) to the people, including Jesus Christ, but that Muhammad was the greatest and final prophet. Muslims follow a set of rules called the Five Pillars of Islam. The first pillar is the *shahada*, or delclaration of faith: "None is to be worshipped [except] Allah: Muhammad is his prophet." The others are *sala* (daily prayer), *zaka* (almsgiving), *saw* (fasting during the holy month of Ramadan), and *hajj* (journeying to Mecca, Islam's sacred city).

About 15.6 percent of Ghana's population are Muslim. Though most Muslims live in northern Ghana, Muslims can be found throughout Ghana.

CHRISTIANITY Christianity arrived in Ghana along with the first Europeans. The Portuguese introduced Roman Catholicism to Ghana in the fifteenth century, just a short time after Islam arrived. But Christianity did not really take hold in the country until the nineteenth century, when Protestant Christian missionaries arrived. Christian religions appealed to many Ghanaians in part because of people like William Wade Harris. Harris was from Liberia, a country to the west of Ghana. He traveled through Ivory Coast and Ghana to share his Christian beliefs and to encourage villagers to form their own churches. European missionaries also attracted members by establishing schools

Kumasi residents attend a **Sunday church service.** The majority of Ghanaians practice some form of Christianity, though many also incorporate animist beliefs and traditions into their practice.

For links to websites where you can find out more about Ghanaian religious traditions, cultural life, current events, cuisine, and much more, visit vgsbooks.com.

for children at a time when there were no secular schools. About 69 percent of Ghanaians are Christian, including Presbyterian, Methodist, Baptist, Anglican, and Mennonite denominations.

Language

English is the official language of Ghana and is widely spoken throughout the country. It is also the official language used in government, large-scale business, national media, and schools. However, each of Ghana's numerous ethnic groups also speaks its own language. In 1962 the government selected nine Ghanaian languages to be used in schools along with English: Akuapem-Twi, Asante-Twi, Dagbane, Dangbe, Ewe, Fanti, Ga, Kasem, and Nzema.

Ghanaian newspapers

Ghana has approximately one hundred indigenous languages that belong to two major language groups, Kwa and Gur. Kwa speakers live in the south and along the coast and include the Akan, Ewe, and Ga-Adangbe. Twi, a Kwa language, is the most widely spoken language in Ghana, and Akan people speak various dialects of it. Fante speak their own language, called Fanti.

Gur speakers live north of the Volta River and include the Grusi, the Gurma, and the Mole-Dagbane. Northern tribes speak many different languages, but most speak a common tongue, Dagbane.

All Ghanaian languages were oral languages, and they were not written down until Christian missionaries arrived in the 1800s. In order to help teach about Christianity and the Bible, the missionaries helped develop written forms of Twi, Fanti, Ga, Ewe, Dagbane, and many other native languages.

Literature

The earliest Ghanaian literature came in the form of oral stories that were passed down through the generations. Most of these stories were moral tales designed to teach children the values of the family and the community in an entertaining way. Many of the traditional stories star Kwaku Ananse, a trickster spider who is smart but naughty. He often gets himself in trouble but saves himself by using his cleverness.

Contemporary Ghana has poets, playwrights, and novelists. Many draw on their rich cultures and personal experiences in their writing.

For example, the author Ayi Kwei Armah was born to Fante parents in Takoradi. Most of his novels deal with the problems of postcolonial Ghana. His first and best-known novel, *The Beautyful Ones Are Not Yet Born*, is about a man who chooses honesty over bribes and corruption, but he and his family suffer for it.

Another Ghanaian author, poet, and playwright, Ama Ata Aidoo, grew up in a Fante royal household. She writes about the contemporary roles of African women and the negative impact of Western influences on African culture. She has also written books for children.

Music and Dance

Music and dancing are central to Ghanaian life and culture. They play a part in the lives of Ghanaians during festivals and celebrations as well as funerals.

Ghanaians play traditional music on many types of instruments, including rattles, drums, horns, and string instruments. Drums are made from wood, gourds, and rawhide. Some drums are used to make music, and some are used as a means of communication. These "talking drums" make sounds that imitate human speech and can be used to send messages and news from village to village.

Drummers parade through the streets of their town, outside of Accra. These drums are made from carved tree trunks with animal skins stretched across the top.

Ewe boys perform a **traditional dance** in their village square.

Traditional dancing is another form of communication. The dances can tell stories or relate events from history. Both men and women dance, and their movements identify them as members of a particular tribe. The Frafra, for example, dance in groups with synchronized stamping movements. The Akan dance with more complex footwork while moving their hands and bodies in intricate patterns. Northern tribes leap, jump, and tumble in their dances.

Ghanaians are also known throughout the world for their vibrant popular music. Highlife music originated in the coastal towns of Ghana in the 1920s and spread from there. This blend of indigenous dance rhythms and melodies and European influences, such as regimental (military) music, sailors' songs, and church hymns, has proved to be one of Africa's most popular forms of music.

Ghana has also developed a lively hip-hop scene. Ghanaian rap is in English as well as a variety of local languages, including Twi, Ga, and Hausa. Lord Kenya is a young rap sensation from Kumasi.

Another form of music is emerging in Ghana. Called hip-life, it is a fusion of highlife and hip-hop. Other types of music heard in Ghana include reggae, gospel, and palm wine, the modern music of the Asante heard mostly in small bars. The musician plays an acoustic guitar and makes up songs about the customers or current events, which are often very funny.

Visual Art and Traditional Crafts

Ghanaian artisans draw on the traditions of their myriad cultures to produce a variety of art forms and styles. Ghana is best known for its dazzling kente cloth. The colorful cloth, made by the Asante and Ewe

A young woman wears a turban, blouse, and skirt made of **kente cloth.**

people of Ghana and Togo, was once worn only by kings. Since the late twentieth century, kente cloth has been the national dress of Ghana and is worn by many.

Asante men and boys weave brightly colored cotton or silk threads by hand into narrow strips. The strips are then sewn together to make fabric. The colors and patterns each have a different meaning and are worn on special occasions, such as the birth of a child or at a funeral, based on the meaning. Gold and yellow, for instance, indicate prosperity, royalty, and eternal life. Green represents bountiful harvest and fertility, blue symbolizes love, and white or ivory is joy. Men drape kente cloth over themselves. Women make skirts, blouses, and head wraps from the cloth.

FASHION COFFINS

In Ghana art is even expressed in coffins. Coffins come in any shape desired, from an airplane to a corn cob to a chicken, depending on the deceased's profession or interests. For example, a farmer might be buried in a corn cob or a pilot in an airplane.

A coffin shaped as a shoe has been fashioned for a shoemaker in Teshi, outside of Accra.

The Ewe also weave kente cloth. Their more geometric patterns are also symbolic and passed down through the generations.

The Asante are also known for their hand-carved stools. Fathers carve stools for their children. People keep their stools their entire lives, and they are seated on them when they are being prepared for burial. Gold and silver cover the stools of royalty and the wealthy.

In the region surrounding Kumasi are four settlements known as the craft villages, each with its particular claim to artistic fame. Bonwire specializes in kente cloth, while Ntonso is famous for Adinkra cloth, which is hand-painted. Ahwiaa specializes in carved figures, including fertility dolls, and Kurofuforum, in the casting of brass.

Sports and Recreation

Soccer is the most popular sport in Ghana. Ghana's national team, the Black Stars, plays at the Accra Sports Stadium to packed stands. The Black Stars take part in important soccer events, such as the African Nations Cup and the World Cup. The Ghanaian women's soccer team, the Black Queens, has a place of equal importance in the international soccer scene. They have twice won second place at the African Women's Championship.

Players battle for the ball during a soccer game in Accra. As in many African countries, soccer is the most popular sport in Ghana.

Ghana has also produced many fine boxers, including Ben Tackie and Azumah Nelson, a three-time World Champion. Other popular sports in Ghana include swimming, tennis, golf, basketball, and cricket. Ghanaians also play a game called *apaat,* which is similar to the British sport of cricket.

Adults and children throughout Ghana play a board game called *oware.* Also known as *mancala,* it is one of the world's oldest games and is popular throughout Africa. It is played with markers, such as small stones, and a wooden board with cups or depressions. Players take turns picking up the markers in a special order until one player collects all the markers and wins.

Oware

Ghanaians in the larger cities have access to many different entertainment venues, including the National Theatre for concerts; the School of Performing Arts at the University of Ghana for drama, poetry, and cultural dancing; and the Executive Film House for Ghanaian and foreign films. Cities offer clubs, discos, restaurants, and pubs. Accra, Tema, and Kumasi also have several Internet cafés.

Ghanaians can watch national TV operated by the Ghana Broadcasting Corporation, as well as satellite, cable, and pay TV. Radios broadcast music and news in English and indigenous languages. Ghana has two national daily papers, *The People's Daily Graphic* and *The Ghanaian Times,* as well as numerous weeklies and privately owned papers.

Food

In the northern part of Ghana, the cycle of extreme dry and wet seasons can make growing and harvesting food difficult. In some years, hunger is a serious threat to many people in the region.

Widespread hunger is not a problem in other parts of Ghana. The fertile soil, mild climates, and good rainfall in the east produce abundant crops and staples for the people in the area and for transport to the cities. The south has a mild climate for good crops and cities where food can be purchased.

The staple foods in Ghana vary from region to region and include yams, corn, plantains, cassava, and cocoyams. Vegetables include okra, eggplants, tomatoes, onions, and the leaves of cocoyams. Common fruits are coconuts, pineapples, and bananas. Groundnuts (peanuts) are an important source of protein, as meat is rare in many Ghanaians' diets. Ghanaians also add fish and beans to stews.

KELEWELE

This spicy snack is made with ripe (yellow) plantains. They are a close relative of the banana but must be cooked before being eaten.

4 plantains (should be firm)
4 tsp. lemon juice
4 tsp. ground ginger

2–4 tsp. cayenne pepper
vegetable oil for frying

1. Peel and slice the plantains into ½-inch-thick rounds and place in a bowl. Sprinkle lemon juice over the pieces and stir to moisten. In a separate bowl, combine the ginger and pepper.
2. Heat about ¼ inch of oil in a heavy skillet until a test piece of plantain sputters. Roll plantain pieces a few at a time in the spice mixture to coat surfaces, then carefully transfer to the skillet. Fry until outsides are crisp and golden, 3–5 minutes.
3. With a slotted spoon, remove plantains to an absorbent cloth or paper towel for cooling slightly. Serve hot. Serves 4 to 6.

Ghanaians usually eat three meals a day. *Waakye* is a popular breakfast or lunch dish made of rice and beans with a spicy sauce of prawns and tomato. Favorite dishes depend on the region, but a common evening meal is *fufu*. Fufu is made of cassava, yam, or plantain that has been boiled, mashed, and formed into balls to be dipped into stew. Stews are a mainstay of meals in Ghana and usually include groundnuts, perhaps some meat or fish, beans, and vegetables.

A group of Ghanaian children eat **fufu** from a communal bowl. Find additional recipes at vgsbooks.com.

Stews are often eaten with *banku,* which is cornmeal that has been cooked and shaped into balls, or *kenkey,* which is made from fermented cornmeal. Ghanaians usually eat with their fingers, using the starch balls as scoops.

Wealthier Ghanaians and tourists eat in restaurants, but most Ghanaians are more likely to eat in cafés, known as "chop houses," or at street stalls. Popular street snacks are *kelewele,* fresh fruit, and coconuts.

Major Holidays and Festivals

Ghana is a country of celebrations and festivals. Important events such as marriage, the naming of a child, puberty rites, and death are marked at family gatherings. Seasonal festivals celebrating harvest or historic events bring a whole ethnic group or clan together. People wear traditional dress and prepare traditional foods. They sing, play drums, and dance, and the whole village is filled with excitement. Central to traditional festivals is the durbar, a procession in which everyone follows the village leaders or chief through the streets to the spot where the festival is to take place.

Ga chiefs remain seated while elders parade by during the Nmayem festival. This festival takes place in the fall and celebrates the harvest.

When babies are born, Ghanaian parents do not take them outside for the first seven days of their life. On the eighth day, they hold a special celebration called an "outdooring ceremony." As part of the ceremony, the child is brought outdoors, officially presented to the community, and the parents receive gifts for the child.

Each of the country's regions has its own major festivals. For the Asante, Akwasidae is an important festival. The Asante religious calendar is broken into nine forty-two-day periods. Each period ends with a festival, culminating in the Akwasidae in the final period of the year. On this day, the Golden Stool is displayed at Manhyia Palace in Kumasi, where the asantehene, or king, lives. People pack the streets to sing and dance.

The yam harvest is celebrated throughout Ghana, particularly by Akan, Ewe, and Ga people. The Ayerye, celebrated by the Fante, marks the initiation of the young men of the tribe into the clan of their fathers. The Ga people living near Accra celebrate Homowo, the harvest festival. Children join in as runners race around the village. The Hogbetsotso festival of the Ewe people of Anlo marks a historical event when the Ewe people escaped a terrible ruler. Damba is celebrated by the Muslims of the upper regions of Ghana to mark the birth of Muhammad.

Homowo celebration

Marriages and funerals bring extended families together. In both, singing, drumming, and dancing play a central role. Marriages celebrate the continuance of life, and funerals honor the beginning of life after death.

Coming-of-age, or puberty, is an important time celebrated by the whole village. It marks the time when boys and girls begin to take on the responsibilities of adulthood. Boys are often circumcised at this time. Girls may be secluded for several weeks while older women teach them about married life. When the girls return to the village, they are eligible for marriage, and in some areas they perform a special dance while the young men watch.

Depending on their religion, Ghanaians also celebrate Christmas, Easter, and other Christian holidays, and Muslim feasts and holy days. Other public holidays include New Year's Day (January 1), Independence Day (March 6), Labor Day (May 1), Republic Day (July 1), and Farmer's Day (early December).

THE ECONOMY

At the time of independence in 1957, Ghana had one of the strongest economies in Africa. But the corruption and huge expenditures of Kwame Nkrumah's government quickly put Ghana in debt. The succession of dishonest civilian and military governments that followed Nkrumah's ousting in 1966 worsened the situation.

During the 1970s and early 1980s, Ghana's economic outlook was bleak. Income from cocoa exports fell as debts, unemployment, and inflation (rising prices combined with a decline in the value of the national currency) skyrocketed, resulting in high prices for food and other staples. Many people left Ghana in search of jobs, but a lot were forced back in 1983 to face a shortage of food, housing, water, and jobs.

Rawlings's government looked to the World Bank and the IMF for loans. Under their guidance, Rawlings's government enacted strict economic reforms, including tight control of spending, elimination of some assistance to farmers, and reduced government controls.

While these changes did result in economic growth rates in excess of 5 percent, high inflation made life even harder for some Ghanaians.

The IMF made the reduction of inflation a major condition for continued financial support. In the 1990s, Ghana's central bank pursued a policy to fight inflation, which had risen dramatically during the previous decade. The reforms successfully resulted in falling inflation and rising economic growth. But the government has also had to deal with the lowering of the value of the cedi (the Ghanaian currency) and public discontent with Ghana's money-saving austerity measures. The political uncertainty of an election year and a depressed cocoa market led to disappointing economic growth in 2000.

In March 2001, the government of Ghana applied for the Enhanced Heavily Indebted Poor Countries (HIPC) Initiative, a World Bank program. The government was able to suspend debt payments to some donors, which brought savings of about $190 million in 2001 alone.

The Ghana Stock Exchange is one of the leading stock exchanges in Africa and has been one of the best performing stock markets among emerging markets in recent years.

In the early 2000s, Ghana's economy seemed to be back on track. Inflation and interest rates were both decreasing to more acceptable levels, and revenue from exports was up. Moderately paced government spending resulted in reduced borrowing.

While challenges remain, Ghana's economy began the 2000s in a relatively strong position. Ghana exported $2.38 billion worth of goods in 2001 and imported $3.78 billion in goods. Main export items are gold, cocoa, timber, tuna, bauxite, aluminum, manganese ore, diamonds, and electricity. The majority of the imports were machinery and equipment, petroleum, and food. Ghana needs to increase the value of its exports to further improve its economy. Trading partners include the United Kingdom, the United States, Germany, and Nigeria.

Ghana has an estimated 9 million people in the workforce, with an average yearly income equivalent to $350 per person. The unemployment rate is around 20 percent. If the government succeeds in creating more jobs and reducing the unemployment rate, the country's economy will also become more stable.

Ghana is a country well endowed with natural resources, and it has twice the value in goods and raw materials per person as the poorer countries in West Africa. But Ghana's total debt stands at more than $6 billion, and the country is heavily dependent on international financial assistance. This means that money that would have been invested elsewhere in the economy must be used to pay down debt.

Agriculture

Ghana's economy centers on agriculture, including fishing and forestry. Agriculture accounts for about 35 percent of the gross domestic product (GDP), the total value of goods and services produced in Ghana in one year. About 60 percent of Ghana's workforce is engaged in agriculture.

The fertile soil and mild climate of central Ghana make it the most productive farming area. By contrast, northern Ghana has infertile soil and unreliable rainfall, leading to poor yields. Across the country, most farms are small and rely on family members to work the soil and harvest the crops. Children begin working on family farms as young as age eleven or twelve.

Ghana has two main types of crops—food crops and cash crops. Food crops, such as cassava, millet, yams, and corn, are grown to be eaten or sold in local markets. Cash crops are grown exclusively to be sold, often overseas. Ghana's main cash crop is cocoa. Other important crops are rice, coffee, peanuts, corn, shea nuts, pineapples, and timber.

Cocoa

Cocoa is the primary ingredient in making chocolate. Ivory Coast is the world's number one cocoa producer, and Ghana ranks number two, supplying more than 12 percent of the world's cocoa. Cocoa alone amounts to 30 percent of Ghana's total exports. About two-thirds of all cocoa products are consumed in Europe and North America, while Africans themselves do not eat much chocolate.

Cacao trees are not native to Ghana. They were introduced by Europeans who brought them from South America. During the colonial period, the British promoted widespread planting of the trees. By 1915 the Gold Coast was the world's leading cocoa producer. Thousands of Ghanaians grew and harvested cocoa beans. But the British government controlled the industry and fixed the price at which it would buy dried

A cacao farmer displays **an unprocessed cacao pod.** Cocoa beans, the raw material from which chocolate is made, are a major cash crop in Ghana.

cocoa beans from farmers. As a result, farmers suffered. In 1947 the Cocoa Marketing Board was established to help farmers receive a fair price for their cocoa beans. But without competition, the board can set the price very low. This means that Ghanaian farmers still are not paid very much for growing and harvesting cocoa beans. In addition, Ghana's income from cocoa is at the mercy of international prices for cocoa. Over the decades, Ghana's cocoa crop has taken some significant hits from disease, bad planning, and competition.

Growing cacao and harvesting the beans is labor intensive. The cacao trees are grown in the forested region of central Ghana that receives heavy rainfall. The land is first cleared of all but a few trees before the cacao trees are planted. The trees are productive after about five years. Harvesting can take three or four months and involves collecting the large, ripe pods, scooping out the beans, and fermenting them. The beans are then sun-dried for about two weeks. Cocoa beans are bitter and must be processed before being turned into chocolate. Processing cocoa produces more money than does growing cacao trees. However, almost all the processing takes place outside of Ghana.

◉ Forestry and Fishing

Forestry is a major industry in rural areas of Ghana. The forests contain valuable hardwoods, such as mahogany and teak. Some areas have sawmills to process the trees into timber before shipping overseas.

Cut timber awaits milling and processing in a small Kumasi lumberyard.

For Ghanaians living along Ghana's rivers, lakes, and coastline, fishing is an important way of earning a living. Off the coast, the waters are rich in tuna, herring, and other fish. Men go out in traditional canoes or motorized boats and bring in the catch, while women process the fish and sell it in markets. Tema has a large commercial tuna-processing plant to which commercial fishermen in Ghana sell their catch. Large, foreign fishing boats compete with the Ghanaian fisherman for this lucrative commodity.

Lake Volta also provides good freshwater fishing, yielding many tons of sardines, mackerel, and other fish. Women often smoke the fish for preservation and sell it in markets.

TOPSOIL

The forests and farmlands of Ghana rely on shallow, fertile topsoil, rather than deep soil. This topsoil is fragile and can easily be destroyed. When the land is cleared of trees, the topsoil can be washed away by heavy rains. If farmers don't allow the soil to rest between plantings, it loses its fertility. The topsoil can become so depleted by this process, called desertification, that eventually nothing will grow there.

Industry

Ghana's industries include mining, lumbering, light manufacturing, aluminum smelting, and food processing. Industrial production grew in the late 1990s and accounted for 25.4 percent of the GDP in 2000. Approximately 20 percent of Ghanaian workers are employed in mining, manufacturing, and industry. Ghana has begun manufacturing some goods that it used to import from developed countries. This industry provides new job opportunities and reduces the amount of money Ghana has to spend buying high-priced goods from abroad. This makes for a more stable economy. Manufactured goods include clothing, cement, plastic goods, and pharmaceuticals.

Workers stack **cement bricks** in a warehouse in Kumasi.

Ghana is one of the most developed countries in Africa, but compared to developed countries such as the United States, it is a poor nation. As in any country, Ghana has rich, middle class, and poor people, but many Ghanaians live in absolute poverty. More than 31 percent of Ghana's population lives below the poverty line.

The majority of Ghana's industries are in the "Golden Triangle," which covers the Asante, Accra, Eastern, and Central regions. Food-processing industries include several cocoa-processing plants where chocolate is made, sugar refineries, flour mills, soft-drink manufacturers, and several small breweries. The timber industry supports sawmills and small furniture- and boat-building factories. Ghana's largest factory is an aluminum-smelting plant in Tema.

Mining

Gold, which first attracted Europeans to the area, remains an important commodity and one of Ghana's major exports. Ghana consistently ranks in the top fifteen gold-producing countries worldwide, and its gold-mining industry employs thousands of workers.

Mining for gold underground has taken place in Ghana since about 1860, when it was controlled by the British. The richest gold mines are located in the Asante region, and some have been operating since the early 1900s. As with cocoa, the price of gold is determined by the world market. If the price of gold falls, Ghana's economy suffers.

Ghana also has other mineral resources, including bauxite; manganese, an ingredient in steel; and diamonds. The diamond mines are located about 70 miles (113 km) northwest of Accra and yield industrial-grade diamonds that are used in drills and metal-cutting machinery.

Aluminum is one of Ghana's important mineral resources.

Services

Service jobs include work in a wide variety of fields, such as retail, health care, government, and tourism. In Ghana, most service jobs are in trade (outdoor market workers) and public service sectors (teachers, doctors, nurses, and government), employing 20 percent of the work force and providing just under 40 percent of the nation's GDP. Tourism is a fast-growing industry for Ghana, and the government has encouraged development of more hotels, restaurants, and attractions including forts, castles, and beaches.

Electricity

The Akosombo Dam and Lake Volta were created to harness the power of water to generate electricity. As a result, Ghana is usually able to generate enough electricity for its own needs. In good years, it can sell extra electricity to the nearby countries of Togo and Benin.

Less electricity is generated in years of little rain. In 1998, for example, drought led to electricity rationing. Power outages had little or no effect on the majority of Ghanaian villagers because most do not have

The energy created by **the Akosombo Dam** supplies Ghana with much of its electricity.

electricity. But in the big cities, traffic lights and streetlights didn't work and small businesses had to cut back on their production and workforce. In addition, the growth of large industries is affected by electricity shortages. Most of the country's electricity is used in Accra, and the biggest single consumer is the Valco Aluminum Company.

In the future, more challenges to Ghana's energy production may arise. Burkina Faso has recently built and proposed more dams on the Volta River system, which may reduce the volume of water reaching the Akosombo Dam, on which Ghana depends for almost all its energy needs.

Transportation

Ghana's avenues of transportation are roads and highways, railways, waterways, and airlines. Ghana's road system suffered during the economic and political turmoil of the 1970s and 1980s. But the government is working on infrastructure development, including the Accra-Kumasi highway. Ghana's 592 miles (953 km) of railways, which extend across the country, are also undergoing rehabilitation.

The Volta, Ankobra, and Tano rivers are navigable. In addition, the creation of Lake Volta has made water transport of goods and people from the north convenient and inexpensive. Ghana also has two coastal ports at Takoradi and Tema for the import and export of goods. The government is dredging Tema harbor to improve its capability. An inland port is planned for Boankra in the Asante region.

Minibuses, often called tro-tros, transport Ghanaians within cities and across the countryside since few people own cars.

Ghana has a total of twelve international and domestic airports in cities and towns including Kumasi, Sunyani, Tamale, and Sekondi-Takoradi. Ghana Airways has international flights from Kotoka International Airport in Accra to almost every country in West Africa as well as New York, London, and other European cities.

The Future

Ghana is a country blessed with natural and mineral resources and fertile land. The country has used its natural resources to improve the quality of life for many of its people, and it has enormous potential for future development.

The Human Development Report is published annually by the United Nations Development Programme and assesses the performance of countries and ranks them using indicators such as life expectancy at birth, adult literacy rate, per capita income, human resource development, and basic needs such as freedom and dignity. In 2002 Ghana moved to 129th place (out of 173 countries), up from 133rd place in 1990.

The strict economic reforms of the past decade have resulted in economic growth, increasing exports, a strong stock market, and more private investment opportunities. If it can maintain its stable political and economic climate and average annual GDP growth rate of nearly 5 percent, Ghana is poised for good economic growth in the twenty-first century.

To achieve widespread economic prosperity, however, Ghana still has some obstacles to overcome. Economic reforms have improved the lives of many, particularly those living in the south and those employed in manufacturing and trade. In rural areas outside of towns and cacao-growing regions, however, is widespread poverty. Life is especially hard in the extreme north, where drought can lead to food shortages and malnutrition.

Potential constraints on Ghana's economic growth include its rapidly growing population and foreign debt created by previous governments. Also, by relying on the export of a few unrefined goods—cocoa and gold—Ghana is vulnerable to fluctuations in their international prices.

Ghana is relatively prosperous compared to many other African nations, but it is still poor compared to Western European nations and the United States. Yet Ghana is rich in tradition and culture, rich in natural resources, and rich in people.

Timeline

1700–1500 B.C.	Kintampo culture exists in the Brong-Ahafo region.
A.D. 300s–1000s	Era of ancient kingdom of Ghana
1200s	Migrations of people into present-day Ghana begin.
1471	Portuguese arrive on Gold Coast.
1481–1482	Portuguese build Elmina Castle.
1500s	Era of slave raids and wars begins.
1598	Dutch arrive in Gold Coast and begin building forts.
1637	Dutch capture Elmina Castle from the Portuguese.
1695	Asante build capital at Kumasi. Beginning of rise and consolidation of Asante Kingdom.
1700s	The Asante Kingdom expands.
1807	British Parliament outlaws the slave trade. The Asante invade the coast.
1850s	Danes leave Ghana.
1860s	Era of slave raids and wars ends.
1872	Dutch pull out, leaving British as sole European power on the Gold Coast.
1874	British attack Kumasi and declare Gold Coast a British Crown Colony.
1877	Seat of colonial government moves from Cape Coast to Accra.
1878	British introduce cacao trees to Ghana.
1902	Northern colonies and Asante Kingdom become part of British protectorate.
1919	All present-day Ghana, including British Togoland, comes under Gold Coast administration.
1927	Achimota College founded in Accra.
1939–1945	Ghanaians serve with the British in World War II.
1947	United Gold Coast Convention (UGCC) founded. UGCC asks Kwame Nkrumah to be its general secretary.
1949	Nkrumah breaks with UGCC and forms the Convention People's Party (CPP).
1950	British leadership jails Nkrumah.
1951	Elections are held under the nation's new constitution. CPP wins two-thirds majority.

1952   Nkrumah becomes prime minister of Gold Coast.

1954   Ghana's new constitution is adopted, granting broad powers to
        Nkrumah's government.

1957   British Colony of the Gold Coast becomes independent Ghana on March 6.

1960   Ghana is declared a republic. Nkrumah becomes Ghana's first president.

1964   Nkrumah declares one-party rule. Akosombo Dam completed.

1966   Nkrumah deposed in a military coup. National Liberation Council seizes power.

1968   Ayi Kwei Armah publishes *The Beautyful Ones Are Not Yet Born.*

1969   New constitution returns Ghana to civilian rule. Progress Party led by Kofi Busia
        comes to power.

1970   Ama Ata Aidoo publishes *No Sweetness Here.*

1972   Colonel Acheampong leads military coup. Nkrumah dies in exile.

1978   Acheampong removed from power in coup led by General Frederick Akuffo.

1979   Junior military officers stage a violent coup on June 4, led by Flight Lieutenant Jerry
        Rawlings. Hilla Limann elected president in July.

1981   Rawlings seizes power again in second coup on December 31. All political parties are
        banned.

1983   Economic reforms introduced with support from the World Bank and International
        Monetary Fund.

1991   Political parties allowed once again.

1992   Voters pass a new constitution forming a multiparty democracy. Rawlings is elected
        president.

1996   Rawlings is reelected.

1998   U.S. president Bill Clinton makes Ghana the first stop on his six-nation tour of
        Africa.

2000   John Kufuor of the New Patriotic Party elected president of Ghana.

2001   Ghanaian Kofi Annan and the United Nations are awarded the Nobel Peace Prize
        for fighting AIDS and terrorism.

2003   Peace talks to end Liberia's civil war are held in Accra.

COUNTRY NAME Republic of Ghana

AREA 92,100 square miles (238,537 sq. km)

MAIN LANDFORMS Kwahu Plateau, Asante Uplands, Volta Basin, Akuapem-Togo Ranges

HIGHEST POINT Mount Afadjato, 2,905 feet (885 m) above sea level

LOWEST POINT Sea level

MAJOR RIVERS Volta River (formed by the White Volta, Black Volta, and Oti), Ankobra, Pra, Tano, Birim, Densu

ANIMALS Bongo antelopes, crocodiles, forest elephants, hippopotamuses, leopards, lions, monkeys

CAPITAL CITY Accra

OTHER MAJOR CITIES Kumasi, Tema, Sekondi-Takoradi, Cape Coast, Elmina, Tamale, Yendi, Bolgatanga

OFFICIAL LANGUAGE English

MONETARY UNIT Cedi. 100 pesewas = 1 cedi.

GHANAIAN CURRENCY

Ghana's official unit of currency is the cedi, which is divided into 100 pesewas. The word *cedi* may come from the Akan word for a small shell, or cowry. These shells were once used as money. Pesewa is from the Akan word *pesewabo,* the dark blue seed of a plant, formerly used as the smallest  gold weight. Ghanaian money comes in 500, 1000, 2000, and 5,000 cedi notes, and coins are 5, 10, 20, 100, and 500. The colorful notes have images of Ghanaians involved in work, such as fishing and harvesting cacao pods.

The Ghanaian flag was first raised when Ghana became an independent nation on March 6, 1957. It was designed by Theodosia Okoh to replace the flag of Britain. The flag has three horizontal stripes of red, gold, and green, with a black five-pointed star in the center of the gold stripe. Red represents the blood of those who died in the struggle for independence, gold symbolizes the country's mineral wealth, and green stands for the rich forests and farms of the country. The star is the symbol of African freedom. Red, gold, and green are the colors of the flag of Ethiopia, Africa's first independent nation. Ghana, like many other African nations, chose to use the same colors when it gained its independence.

The lyrics of Ghana's national anthem were first written by a government committee in 1956. The music was written by Ghanaian composer and musician Philip Gbeho at the same time. The lyrics were revised in 1966, after a coup by the National Liberation Council. Below is the first verse of the anthem, "Hail the Name of Ghana."

"Hail the Name of Ghana"

God bless our homeland Ghana,
And make our nation great and strong,
Bold to defend for ever
The cause of Freedom and of Right.
Fill our hearts with true humility,
Make us cherish fearless honesty,
And help us to resist oppressors' rule
With all our will and might for evermore.

For a link where you can listen to Ghana's national anthem, "Hail the Name of Ghana," go to vgsbooks.com.

FREDDY ADU (b. 1989) Adu is an up-and-coming soccer player who was born in Tema. He learned the game as a very young child and immigrated to the United States at age eight. In early 2002, he was recruited to attend a special high school for gifted soccer players. He signed with D.C. United, a U.S. major league soccer team, in 2003.

AMA ATA AIDOO (b. 1942) Aidoo is a poet, playwright, and author of books for adults and children. She writes about the contemporary roles of African women and the negative impact of Western influences on African culture. She was born Christina Ama Aidoo in 1942 in Abeadzi Kyiakor in south-central Ghana.

KOFI ATTA ANNAN (b. 1938) Annan is the seventh secretary-general of the United Nations (UN). He is the first black African to hold the job and he and the UN were jointly awarded the 2001 Nobel Peace Prize for their efforts in fighting AIDS and terrorism while promoting a peaceful world. Annan was born in Kumasi on April 8, 1938, and studied at the University of Science and Technology in Kumasi, as well as at Macalester College in Minnesota and at the Massachusetts Institute of Technology. He began his career at the UN in 1962 and has led difficult diplomatic assignments during his tenure. These assignments include the release of Western hostages in Iraq during the Persian Gulf War (1991) and the transition in Bosnia-Herzegovina from from military oversight by UN peacekeeping forces to North Atlantic Treaty Organization (NATO) troops. In July 2002, he was unanimously reelected by the UN General Assembly to a second five-year term.

AYI KWEI ARMAH (b. 1939) Armah is the author of five novels, most dealing with the problems of postcolonial Ghana. His best-known novel is *The Beautyful Ones Are Not Yet Born.* He was born in 1939 in Takoradi to Fante parents and studied at the Groton School and Harvard University in Massachusetts.

YAA ASANTEWAA (ca. 1850–1920) A leader of the Edweso State (an area under Asante control), her official title was Edwesohemaa (Queen Mother of Edweso) Yaa Asantewaa. In 1900 she mobilized Asante warriors to attack the British fort at Kumasi in an effort to drive them from the Asante Kingdom. When the Asante efforts failed, British soldiers at the fort captured her and sent her into exile.

LORD KENYA (b. 1978) Lord Kenya is a popular young rap singer from Kumasi. He was born to a Nzema father and an Asante mother who named him Abraham Philip Akpor Kojo Kenya. He won the hip-life Album of the Year at the 2001 Ghana Music Awards and Best Ghanaian Rap Award at the 2000 Anansekrom Festival in Canada.

JOHN AGYEKUM KUFUOR (b. 1938) Kufuor (also spelled Kuffuor) won the presidential elections in December 2000 and was sworn in as president of Ghana on January 9, 2001. Kufuor was born in Kumasi on December 8, 1938, and studied at Prempeh College, later earning a master's degree in law from Oxford University in England. He has more than thirty years of experience in public service, including terms as a member of parliament and deputy minister of foreign affairs.

E. T. MENSAH (1919–1996) Mensah was a Ghanaian musician who pioneered the development of the swing-jazz–influenced highlife dance bands popular throughout West Africa. He is often called the "King of Highlife." He was born in Accra.

AZUMAH NELSON (b. 1958) Nelson began his boxing career in 1979. In 1984 he won the World Featherweight title, and in 1988 the Junior Lightweight title. Nelson regained the title in 1995 at the age of thirty-seven, when most people felt he was too old for boxing. He became known as "The Professor" because he fought as well as taught younger boxers. He retired at age thirty-nine and is considered one of the greatest boxers to come out of the African continent. He was born in Accra.

KWAME NKRUMAH (1909–1972) Born in the village of Nkroful in southwestern Ghana, Nkrumah formed the Convention People's Party in 1949 and led the country to independence. He was the first prime minister of the Gold Coast and, when Ghana became a republic in 1960, its first president. Nkrumah was overthrown in a military coup in 1966. He lived the rest of his life in exile in Guinea. President Sékou Touré of Guinea made Nkrumah Guinea's honorary president.

JERRY JOHN RAWLINGS (b. 1947) Rawlings was born in Accra on June 22, 1947. As a young military officer, he led successful coups in 1979 and 1981. He dissolved Ghana's constitution and set up the provisional National Defense Council with himself as chairman. Rawlings focused on ending corruption in government (often by violent means) and improving the economy. He won the presidency in a multiparty democratic election in 1992 and was reelected in 1996. Ghanaian law forbade him from seeking a third term. Since then, Rawlings has worked on campaigns to contain the spread of HIV/AIDS, particularly in Africa, and has volunteered as Eminent Person for the United Nations International Year of Volunteers (2001).

OSEI TUTU (ca. 1660–1717) In the late 1600s, Osei Tutu united five smaller states and became the first asantehene of the Asante Kingdom. He built the Asante capital at Kumasi and established the Golden Stool as a symbol of the king's power. He was born in Kumasi.

ANOKYE SWORD A sword-shaped rock sticks out of the ground in Kumasi, where according to legend, the Golden Stool descended from the heavens. The Asante say that if the sword is pulled out of the ground, their kingdom with disappear.

BOABENG-FIEMA MONKEY SANCTUARY This sanctuary in the Brong-Ahafo region is home to many varieties of forest monkeys, including black-and-white colobus monkeys and Campbell's Mona monkeys.

CAPE COAST CASTLE This castle, built in 1652, grew from a small trading fort to become the Gold Coast's second largest slave trading post. It includes a museum that tells its gruesome history.

DIGYA NATIONAL PARK Located in the Volta region, Digya is Ghana's second-largest protected area and is known for its bush pigs, water buck, crocodiles, and manatees.

ELMINA CASTLE Built by the Portuguese west of modern-day Cape Coast in 1482, Elmina Castle was the first fort on the Gold Coast. It was later expanded to become the largest slave trading post. Slaves were kept here before being put on ships for transport.

INDEPENDENCE SQUARE The Eternal Flame of African Liberation burns at this public square in Accra, also known as Black Star Square. Independence Day ceremonies are held at the square every March 6.

LAKE VOLTA This lake is one of the world's largest artificially created lakes. Activities here include a visit to the Akosombo Dam, fishing, and boating.

LARABANGA MOSQUE Believed to be the oldest mosque in Ghana, Larabanga is an example of Sudanese (north African) architecture. It is located in northern Ghana.

MAKOLA MARKET This famous Accra market is one of Africa's most colorful markets. Food, medicine, shoes, and tools are among the items sold here.

MANHYIA PALACE This Kumasi museum is home of the asantehene and the Golden Stool. The palace is open to visitors.

MOLE NATIONAL PARK Ghana's best-known park is home to lions, leopards, and more than three hundred species of birds.

NATIONAL CULTURE CENTRE This Kumasi complex includes a museum of Asante history, a library, an exhibition hall, and an excellent craft shop.

NATIONAL MUSEUM In this Accra museum, a collection of ancient relics, documents, and pictures show the history of Ghana.

Adinkra cloth: handwoven cloth printed with Asante symbols

animism: the belief that inanimate objects and forces of nature have conscious life

asantehene: Asante king

coup: the forceful overthrow or change in government by a small group. When a coup is carried out without injuries or deaths, it is called a bloodless coup.

desertification: the transformation of arable land (land fit for growing crops) into desert. When farmers overuse a plot of land, it can lose its fertility to the extent that vegetation (plants) will no longer grow there and the land becomes desert.

durbar: a parade through a Ghanaian village at the beginning of a festival to honor the leaders

gross domestic product (GDP): a measure of the total value of goods and services produced within a country in a certain amount of time (usually one year). A similar measurement is gross national product (GNP). GDP and GNP are often measured in terms of purchasing power parity (PPP). PPP converts values to international dollars, making it possible to compare how much similar goods and services cost to the residents of different countries.

harmattan: a dry, dusty wind that blows southward from the Sahara

inflation: a sharp and continuing rise in the price of goods

Islam: a religion founded on the Arabian Peninsula in the seventh century A.D. by the prophet Muhammad. It was introduced to Ghana in the 1400s. Approximately 15 percent of modern Ghanaians practice Islam.

kente cloth: traditional handwoven cloth originally made for Asante royalty

matrilineal: tracing family descent through the mother and her female ancestors. The Akan people of Ghana have matrilineal societies.

Muslim: a follower of Islam

parliament: a national representative body with legislative power. Members of parliament are elected by voters.

protectorate: a political until dependent on a stronger power for its economic and territorial welfare

savanna: a flat, almost treeless grassland

Glossary

Angelou, Maya. *All God's Children Need Traveling Shoes.* **New York: Random House, 1986.**
This segment of Angelou's autobiography takes place in Ghana in the early 1960s, and it includes the story of Angelou's visit to Keta, where she discovers her roots.

Appiah, Kwame Anthony. *In My Father's House: Africa in the Philosophy of Culture.* **New York: Oxford University Press, 1992.**
Written by a philosopher, this is a collection of essays on race and culture. The author shares his reflections on being the child of an African father and an English mother, and growing up in Ghana and later living abroad.

Berry, LaVerle, ed. *Ghana: A Country Study.* **3rd ed. Washington, D.C.: Federal Research Division, Library of Congress, 1995.**
Website: <http://lcweb2.loc.gov/frd/cs/ghtoc.html> (September 9, 2003).
This book is a good source for information about Ghanaian political, economic, social, and cultural institutions. It was written by a team of social scientists. The entire book is also available online.

Brace, Steve. *Ghana: A Study of an Economically Developing Country.* **New York: Thomson Learning, 1995.**
This book provides an excellent overview of Ghana's economy, standard of living, and culture. It was written for young readers.

Central Intelligence Agency. "Ghana." *The World Factbook 2002.* **2002.**
Website: <http://www.cia.gov/cia/publications/factbook/geos/gh.html> (September 9, 2003).
This website provides a general profile of Ghana, produced by the Central Intelligence Agency. The profile includes brief summaries of the nation's geography, people, government, economy, communications, and transportation.

Check, Erika. "The Silence of the Woods." *Newsweek* **136, no. 20, November 13, 2000, 65.**
This article focuses on the disappearance of primates in West Africa and discusses the Miss Waldron's red colobus monkey in Ghana.

Chocolate, Debbi. *Kente Colors.* **New York: Walker and Company, 1996.**
This book provides information on meanings of colors and patterns in kente cloth. It includes color paintings.

Edgerton, Robert. B. *The Fall of the Asante Empire: The Hundred-Year War for Africa's Gold Coast.* **New York: The Free Press, 1995.**
This book gives an in-depth look at the century-long conflict between the British and the Asante.

The Embassy of Ghana. **N.d.**
Website: <http://www.ghana-embassy.org> (September 9, 2003).
This is a good site for Ghanaian statistics, a government profile, trade and economic issues, and tourism. It includes a nice slide show of interesting places to visit.

The Europa World Year Book 2001. London: Europa Publications Limited, 2001.

This is an annual publication that covers the recent history, economy, and government of most world countries, including Ghana, as well as providing a wealth of statistics on population, employment, trade, and more. A short directory of offices and organizations is also included.

"Ghana." *Lonely Planet.* N.d.
Website: <http://www.lonelyplanet.com/destinations/africa/ghana> (September 9, 2003).

This site, designed for travelers, contains a wealth of information on attractions, events, and activities, particularly in Accra and Kumasi.

Ghana Home Page. September 9, 2003.
Website: <http://www.ghanaweb.com> (September 9, 2003)

This website is a comprehensive resource on the country. It includes tons of information on all things Ghanaian, including current news, famous people, economic issues, gossip, sports, classifieds, demographic statistics, and jokes.

Hayden, Thomas. "Safaris and Sensitivity." *Newsweek* 135, no. 23, June 5, 2000, 56.

This article contains information on ecotourism in West Africa.

Levy, Patricia. *Cultures of the World: Ghana.* New York: Marshall Cavendish, 1999.

Written for young readers, this book gives a good overview of all aspects of Ghana and Ghanaian culture. It includes many color photos of children.

Mann, Kenny. *Ghana, Mali, Songhay: The Western Sudan.* New York: Dillon Press, 1996.

This book contains a history of these three great kingdoms, written for grades six and above. It also features stories and myths that were part of these ancient cultures. It includes many color photos and illustrations.

McKissack, Patricia, and Fredrick McKissack. *The Royal Kingdoms of Ghana, Mali, and Songhay.* New York: Henry Holt, 1994.

This book gives deep but concise coverage of the ancient kingdoms of West Africa. It includes black-and-white photos.

Provincial, Francis, and Catherine McNamara. *A Child's Day in a Ghanaian City.* New York: Benchmark Books, 2001.

This book follows seven-year-old Nii Kwei as he attends school in Accra and goes about his daily chores and activities.

The Republic of Ghana. September 9, 2003.
Website: <http://www.ghana.gov.gh> (September 9, 2003).

This is the official Ghanaian government site, and it is a good source for official statistics, history, culture, demographics, and news highlights.

Turner, Barry. *The Statesman's Yearbook: The Politics, Cultures and Economies of the World.* New York: Palgrave Macmillan Ltd., 2002.

This resource provides concise information on Ghanaian history, government, economy, climate, and culture, including relevant statistics.

Annan, Kofi. *We the Peoples.* **New York: Ruder Finn Press, 2002.**
This book contains the full text of Kofi Annan's Nobel Peace Prize lecture, delivered in Oslo, Norway, on December 10, 2001.

Appiah, Peggy. *Tales of an Ashanti Father.* **Boston: Beacon Press, 1989.**
This book includes twenty-two folktales from Ghana, several featuring Kwaku Ananse, the trickster spider.

Barnett, Jeanie M. *Ghana.* **Major World Nations. Philadelphia: Chelsea House Publishers, 1999.**
This book gives a thorough introduction to the history, geography, politics, government economy, natural resources, education, people, and culture of Ghana.

Blauer, Ettagalie, and Jason Lauré. *Ghana.* **Enchantment of the World. Chicago: Children's Press, 1999.**
Text and full-color photographs cover the history and contemporary life of the people of Ghana.

Davis, Lucy. *Ghana.* **Countries of the World. Mankato, MN: Bridgestone Books, 1999.**
This book offers an introduction to the geography, history, natural resources, culture, and people of Ghana.

Hamilton, Janice. *Ivory Coast in Pictures.* **Minneapolis: Lerner Publications Company, 2004.**
This book examines the history, government, economy, people, geography, and cultural life of Ghana's French-speaking western neighbor.

Kite, L. Patricia. *Maya Angelou.* **Minneapolis: Lerner Publications Company, 1998.**
This biography of the multifaceted African American woman, Maya Angelou, traces her life from her childhood in the segrated South to her prominence as a well-known writer.

Littlefield, Holly. *Colors of Ghana.* **Minneapolis: Lerner Publications Company, 1999.**
A discussion of colors introduces young readers to landmarks and important cultural information about Ghana.

Nabwire, Constance, and Bertha Vining Montgomery. *Cooking the West African Way.* **Minneapolis: Lerner Publications Company, 2002.**
This cookbook provides cultural information as well as step-by-step instructions for making some of the tastiest and most popular dishes in West Africa, including sweet potato fritters and a corn dish from Ghana.

News in Ghana. **September 8, 2003.**
Website: <http://www.newsinghana.com>
This site offers top news stories in Ghana and links to other news sources.

Further Reading and Websites

Strand, Paul. Ghana: *An African Portrait.* **New York: Aperture, Inc., 1976.**

This book contains wonderful photos and personal reflections that provide insight into life in Ghana.

Temko, Florence. *Traditional Crafts from Africa.* **Minneapolis: Lerner Publications Company, 1996.**

This book describes hands-on crafts projects for kids. Each project is based on the craft from an African country. One project tells how to make Adinkra cloth.

vgsbooks.com
Website: <http://www.vgsbooks.com>

Visit vgsbooks.com, the home page of the Visual Geography Series®, which is updated regularly. You can get linked to all sorts of useful on-line information, including geographical, historical, demographic, cultural, and economic websites. The vgsbooks.com site is a great resource for late-breaking news and statistics.

Index

Accra, 5, 13, 16–17, 19, 26, 27, 31, 34, 36, 37, 40, 41, 51, 52, 62, 63, 64, 65, 66, 67, 68, 71, 72
Afadjato, Mount, 9, 68
African Company of Merchants, 26
African Union, 30
agriculture, 7, 9, 13, 15, 16, 18, 20, 37, 39, 40, 52, 58–59
Aidoo, Ama Ata, 48, 67, 70
Angelou, Maya, 40
animism, 44–45, 46, 73. *See also* religion
Annan, Kofi, 33, 67, 70
architecture, 72
Arden-Clarke, Charles, 29
Armah, Ayi Kwei, 48, 67, 70
Armed Forces Revolutionary Council (AFRC), 31
art and visual artists, 44, 49–51
Asante. *See* ethnic groups
authors, 47–48. *See also* Aidoo, Ama Ata; Angelou, Maya; Armah, Ayi Kwei

Burkina Faso, 8, 42, 63

cacao and cocoa, 7, 9, 15, 18, 19, 27, 30, 37, 39, 56, 57, 58, 59–60, 62, 65, 66, 68
Center for Scientific Research into Plant Medicine, 42
Christianity, 5, 26, 44, 46–47, 55. *See also* religion
cities, 13, 16–19, 20, 37, 41, 43, 52, 63, 65, 68. *See also* Accra, Kumasi, Sekondi, Takoradi, Tema
climate, 12–13, 52, 58
Columbus, Christopher, 22
Convention People's Party (CPP), 28, 66, 71
crafts, 51
currency, 32, 56, 57, 68

dance, 48, 49, 52, 54, 55
Digya National Park, 15, 72
domestic challenges, 7, 16, 40, 41, 43, 52, 58, 65

economy, 34, 56–65
ecotourism. *See* tourism

education, 17, 18, 19, 26, 27, 37, 42–43, 47, 52, 66
electricity. *See* energy
employment, 7, 56, 58–59, 61
energy, 11, 15, 37, 63–64
Enhanced Heavily Indebted Poor Countries (HIPC) Initiative, 57
ethnic groups, 4, 5, 16, 22, 26, 30, 38–40, 45, 47, 54; Asante, 4, 7, 18, 22, 24–26, 38–40, 49, 50, 51, 55, 66, 70, 71, 72, 73; Ewe, 38, 39, 40, 49, 51, 55; Ga-Adangbe, 39–40
Ewe. *See* ethnic groups

families, 36–37, 38, 40, 45, 54, 55
fishing, 11, 40, 61, 68, 72
flag, 69
flora and fauna, 13–15, 16, 45, 68, 72
food, 16, 37, 52–54, 56, 58, 65, 72; recipe, 53
foreign trade, 7, 15, 16, 58, 59, 62, 64, 65
forestry, 60
forests, 8, 9, 13–14, 15, 61, 69

Ga-Adangbe. *See* ethnic groups
Ghana: boundaries, location, and size, 4, 8; currency, 32, 56, 57, 68; flag, 69; maps, 6, 10; national anthem, 69; regions, 35, 40, 42, 44, 52, 53, 54, 62, 64, 72
gold. *See* mineral wealth
government, 34–35, 47
gross domestic product (GDP), 58, 73

Harris, William Wade, 46
health, 17, 37, 40–42
history: ancient, 20, 66; arrival of Europeans, 4, 16, 19, 22–23, 39, 46, 62, 66; Asante Kingdom, 18, 25, 26, 39; British rule, 4, 5, 16, 26–28, 59, 62, 66, 67; early migrants, 22; Ghana Empire, 4, 5, 20–22; independence, 5, 29, 30, 43, 56, 67, 69, 71; modern, 28–34, 66–67; slave trade, 4, 16, 21, 23–25, 26, 39, 66, 72
HIV/AIDS, 42, 71. *See also* health
holidays and festivals, 18, 44, 48, 54–55

industry, 17, 61–65
inflation, 56, 57, 58
Islam, 5, 21, 22, 37, 44, 46, 55, 72, 73. *See also* religion
Ivory Coast, 4, 8, 16, 46, 59

Kakum National Park, 14–15, 16
Kufour, John, 33, 34, 40, 67, 70
Kumasi, 12, 16, 18, 25, 26, 27, 36, 37, 40, 43, 46, 49, 51, 52, 55, 61, 64, 65, 66, 70, 71, 72
Kwahu Plateau, 8, 9, 11, 12, 13, 68

language, 38, 43, 47, 49, 52, 68
literature, 44, 47–48

manufacturing, 61–62
maps, 6, 10
matrilineal society, 39
media, 47, 52
Mensah, E. T., 70
mineral wealth, 4, 15, 18, 21, 22, 23, 24, 26, 30, 39, 58, 62, 65, 69. *See also* mining
mining, 16, 18, 27, 61, 62
Mole National Park, 15, 72
music, 44, 48, 49, 52, 54, 55, 70
musical instruments, 44–45, 48, 49, 54, 55

national anthem, 69
National Culture Centre, 18, 25, 72
natural resources, 7, 15–16, 26, 58, 65. *See also* fishing; flora and fauna; forests; mineral wealth; tropical rain forest
Nelson, Azumah, 52, 71
Nkrumah, Kwame, 28–29, 30, 56, 66, 67, 71

population, 9, 16, 19, 36, 38, 39, 40, 42, 45, 46, 58, 65
poverty. *See* domestic challenges
Provisional National Defense Council (PNDC), 31, 71

Rawlings, Jerry, 31–33, 56, 67, 71
regions, 35, 40, 42, 44, 52, 53, 54, 62, 64
religion, 5, 21, 37, 39, 44–46, 55

rivers, 11, 12, 14, 61, 64, 68. *See also* Volta River system

savanna, 8, 9, 11, 13, 14, 16, 22
Sekondi, 16, 19, 65
services, 63
slave trade, 4, 16, 21, 23–25, 26, 39, 66, 72
soccer, 5, 17, 51
sports and recreation, 51–52, 71. *See also* soccer

Takoradi, 13, 19, 48, 64, 65, 70
Tema, 16, 19, 20, 52, 61, 62, 64
Togo, 4, 8, 9, 50, 63
tourism, 16, 54
transportation, 17, 27, 64–65
tropical rain forest, 9, 13, 14

United Gold Coast Convention (UGCC), 28, 29, 66

Volta, Lake, 11–12, 61, 63, 64, 72
Volta River system, 9, 11, 12, 20, 22, 47, 63, 64, 68
voodoo, 39, 80

writers. *See* authors

Captions for photos appearing on cover and chapter openers:

Cover: In a village in central Ghana, the bones of sacrificed animals hang from an ancestral shrine, known as a *tengani*, behind rows of conical chicken coops. Some Ghanaians practice voodoo, a religion that can involve animal sacrifice and trancelike dancing.

pp. 4–5 This girl lives in northern Ghana.

pp. 8–9 The Akuapem–Togo Ranges lie north of Ghana's coastal plain. Mount Gemi is a minor peak in this range.

pp. 36–37 Ghanaian children congregate in a local market after school.

pp. 44–45 Drummers and percussionists from the Ewe people thump out a rhythm on a beach in southern Ghana. Drumming is an important part of Ghanaian culture.

pp. 56–57 Near Kumasi a farmworker spreads cocoa beans on a table to dry in the sun.

Photo Acknowledgments
The images in this book are used with the permission of: © George Georgiou/Panos Pictures, pp. 4-5; Digital Cartographics, pp. 6, 10; © Trip/M. Barlow, pp. 8-9, 47, 64; © Liba Taylor/Panos Pictures, pp. 11 (top), 18 (top); © Victor Englebert, pp. 11 (bottom), 12, 15, 17, 18 (bottom), 38, 39 (bottom), 41 (bottom), 44-45, 46, 51, 53, 56-57; © Trip/J. Sweeney, p. 13; © Michele Burgess, p. 14 (top); © Jason Lauré, pp. 14 (bottom), 50 (bottom), 62; © Jak Kilby, pp. 19, 49; © Trip/J. Highet, pp. 23, 39 (top), 50 (top); Musée Royal de L'Afrique Centrale, p. 24; Library of Congress, pp. 27, 28, 29; © Bettmann/CORBIS, p. 31; © Robert Patrick/CORBIS Sygma, p. 32; © UN/DPI/CORBIS SYGMA, p, 33; © AFP/CORBIS, p. 34; © Trip/M Jelliffe, pp. 36-37; © Betty Press/Panos Pictures, pp. 41 (top), 59, 63; © Trip/B. Seed, pp. 43, 48, 54; © Giacomo Pirozzi/Panos Pictures, p. 52; © Caroline Penn/Panos Pictures, pp. 60, 61; © Todd Strand/Independent Picture Service, p. 68; Laura Westlund, p. 69.

Cover photo: © Margaret Courtney-Clarke/CORBIS. Back cover photo: NASA.